5-24-01

CAMBRIAN INTELLIGENCE

· ·

CAMBRIAN INTELLIGENCE

. . . .

The Early History of the New AI

RODNEY A. BROOKS

A Bradford Book
The MIT Press
Cambridge, Massachusetts
London, England

This book was set in Computer Modern by the author using LaTeX and was printed and bound in the United States of America.

Library of Congress Cataloging-in-Publication Data

Brooks, Rodney Allen.
    Cambrian intelligence: the early history of the new AI /
    Rodney A. Brooks.
        p. cm.
    "A Bradford Book."
    Includes bibliographical references.
    ISBN 0-262-02468-3 (hc.: alk. paper)–0-262-52263-2
    (pbk.: alk. paper)
    1. Robotics. 2. Artificial intelligence. I. Title.
    TJ211.B695 1999
    629.8'9263–dc21

                                                    99-17220
                                                    CIP

Contents

Preface
· ·

This is a collection of scientific papers and essays that I wrote from 1985 to 1991, a period when the key ideas of behavior-based robotics were developed. Behavior-based robotics has now been widely adopted for mobile robots of all sorts on both Earth and Mars.

Mobile robotics was an almost non-existent curiosity fourteen years ago. There were many unmanned guided vehicles developed to carry parts in automated manufacturing plants, but they just had to follow guide wires in the ground. In contrast, autonomous mobile robots are conceived of as robots that can operate in worlds where the layout of obstacles are not known ahead of time; they are to operate in the sorts of worlds that people and animals can negotiate with ease. The few autonomous mobile robots that did exist fourteen years ago were pro- grammed to build elaborate three-dimensional world models and to *plan* a long series of actions within those world models before they started to move. Out of necessity the handful of researchers in the area made a restriction that their robots could operate only in static worlds.

The behavior-based approach to mobile robots changed the way robots were programmed, at least at the lower levels of control. The eight chapters of this book are papers that I wrote (one with a student) introducing the behavior-based approach; four are technical papers de- scribing robot systems and approaches, and four are philosophical pa- pers describing the changes in intellectual point of view that enables this approach.

In an idealized scientific world one might think that the new intel- lectual point of view was developed first and then the technology and technicians caught up and implemented systems guided by those new intellectual points of view. But that is certainly not the way things developed for me. In all cases the technological implementations came first, and the philosophical realizations followed later. For this reason the technical papers are presented first and the philosophical papers second. However, either part of the book can be read first as all the papers were written to be read as single works. Philosophers may safely

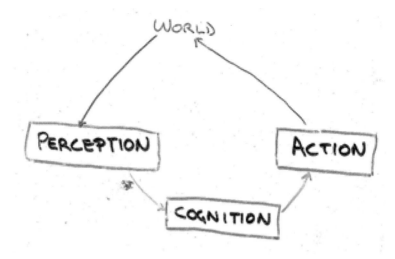

Figure 1: The traditional model where cognition mediates between perceptions and plans of actions.

skip the technical papers without finding themselves ungrounded in the philosophical sections.

While technology definitely led philosophy there was one key earlier realization, philosophical in nature, that was critical to the development of the behavior-based approach. In hindsight, it may seem to be the critical realization that enabled and outlines the whole approach but I must say that the new approach was not at all obvious at the time of the realization.

The realization was that the so-called central systems of intelligence — or *core AI* as it has been referred to more recently — was perhaps an unnecessary illusion, and that all the power of intelligence arose from the coupling of perception and actuation systems. This is the cornerstone of behavior-based robotics, both mobile robots as they have developed over the last twelve years and humanoid robots that have been developed more recently.

For me this realization came about after spending a number of years working on both perception, mostly vision-based perception, and motion planning, mostly for abstract two-dimensional shapes and some for robot manipulator arms.

I had always assumed that there would be some intelligent system coupling the two of them together doing so-called *high-level reasoning*. Indeed this was the generally accepted order of things, largely validated by the early successes of the Shakey robot at the SRI Artificial Intelligence Center in Menlo Park, California, near Stanford University. The higher-level reasoning system of Shakey worked in predicate logic, and the perception system produced descriptions of the world in first-order predicate calculus. However, that work in the late sixties and very early seventies was carried out in a very restricted world; a well-lit area consisting of only matte-painted walls, clean floors, and large cubes and wedges with each face painted a different color. These restrictions made the vision problem fairly straightforward though not trivial.

By the early eighties it seemed to me that if there was to be any validity to this approach then computer vision should be able to deliver predicate calculus descriptions of much less constrained and much more complex worlds. Computer vision systems ought to be able to operate in the ordinary sorts of environments that people operated in, cluttered offices with things stuck on walls and disorderly piles of papers that partially obscured objects. A computer monitor, for instance, should be visually recognizable as such even if it were a new model with a shape and size slightly different from all those that the vision system had been told about or had seen before. Even more challenging, a computer vision system should be able to operate outdoors and pick out trees, hills, pathways, curbs, houses, cars, trucks, and everything else that a three-year-old child could name.

There were no vision systems around doing anything even remotely as sophisticated. Any such dreams had been put on hold by the computer vision community as they worked on very difficult but much simpler challenges. But even so, the validity of the approach was not questioned. Rather, the progress in computer vision was questioned. Alex (Sandy) Pentland, then a young researcher at SRI held a weekly seminar series to try to uncover the sources of the seeming stall in computer vision. The title of the seminar series was *From Pixels to Predicates*, setting the tone for the direction of inquiry. I was a very junior faculty member at Stanford at the time and was invited to give one of the weekly talks during the 1983–84 academic year.

I have kept my crude hand-drawn opening slides from that talk, and they are reproduced in figures 1 and 2. I did not have a cogent argument to make based on these slides. It may have been that I had recently discovered the joy of brashly telling everyone that their most implicit beliefs or assumptions were wrong, or at least open to question; the central systems people were giving us perception people a hard time that we just weren't producing the sorts of outputs that would enable their *intelligent* systems to do all the really hard stuff. Or it may have been that I was extraordinarily frustrated both with the difficulty of producing complete descriptions of the world from visual input, and with the immense complexity that had to be maintained in such models of the world in order to plan successful motor actions within them. Or I may have had an incredibly clever insight. I doubt the latter, and think it was a combination of the first two, perhaps dominated by the perverse pleasure of the first one.

In any case there were actually three transparencies. An underlying one and two overlays that gave rise to the two different figures. The underlying transparency had the words PERCEPTION, WORLD, and AC- TION written on them, with two arrows, one from action to the world, and one from the world to perception, indicating the causality chain of the model. The first overlay gave the image reproduced in figure 1. In this, COGNITION was the thing, the computational box, that was used to decipher perceptions and to order up actions. This was very much the common implicitly held view of how to build an intelligent system, and was certainly the approach implicitly promoted by Sandy's semi- nar. The basic idea is that perception goes on by itself, autonomously producing world descriptions that are fed to a cognition box that does all the real *thinking* and instantiates the real *intelligence* of the system. The thinking box then tells the action box what to do, in some sort of high-level action description language.

In my talk I then changed the overlay to give the image in figure 2. This completely turns the old approach to intelligence upside down. It denies that there is even a box that is devoted to cognitive tasks. Instead it posits both that the perception and action subsystems do all the work and that it is only an external observer that has anything to do with cognition, by way of attributing cognitive abilities to a system that works well in the world but has no explicit place where cognition is done.

The first model has the recursive problem of deciding what is in the cognition box, and perhaps finding yet another little homunculus inside there until eventually all the power of reason is reduced to a rather dumb little computational intelligence operating in such highly abstract terms that there is no real place for truly intelligent action to be generated. Rather, it is slightly dressed up and made more real as each level of recursion is unwound.

The second model solves this whole problem by denying its existence. Of course, I had absolutely no idea at the time how to blend the percep- tual and actuator systems to work together and to achieve all the desired behaviors. And there was certainly no hint of it in the actual paper I contributed to an edited book on the series that Sandy produced.

In retrospect, my students and I have spent the last fourteen years trying to justify that second figure, by building ever more complex arti- facts which demonstrate intelligent behavior using the second model.

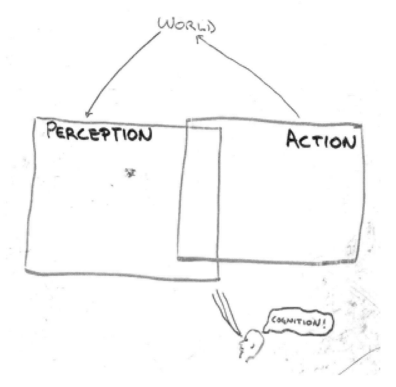

Figure 2: The new model, where the perceptual and action subsystems are all there really is. Cognition is only in the eye of an observer.

The eight papers in this book represent my contributions to the development of the behavior-based approach to robotics. This approach has now achieved success across two planets. Hundreds of people are developing new applications using the approach; applications in entertainment, service industries, agriculture, mining, and the home. There is a real chance that these developments will soon bring about yet another change in humanity's relationship with machines following our earlier agricultural, industrial, and information revolutions: the robot revolution.

Acknowledgments

I have had many students over the years who have contributed to the formation of my ideas and helped with the technological implementations. Those who worked with me during the period that this book covers include Phil Agre, Colin Angle, Cynthia Breazeal (Ferrell), David Chapman, Mike Ciholas, Jon Connell, Peter Cudhea, Anita Flynn, Chris Foley, Ian Horswill, Peter Ning, Pattie Maes, Maja Mataric, Lynne Parker, and Paul Viola.

A number of my colleagues at the MIT Artificial Intelligence Laboratory have been useful sounding boards, and sometimes I have even convinced them of my arguments. Those that I harassed during the times of these papers include Eric Grimson, Tomás Lozano-Pérez, David Kirsh, and Thomas Marill.

There were other colleagues who directly helped me with these ideas, including Leslie Kaelbling, Grinnell More, and Stan Rosenschein.

Annika Pfluger has assisted me daily for many years, and she was very active in bringing this volume to fruition, both with the references and the figures.

Cambridge, Massachussets
March, 1999

PART I

....

TECHNOLOGY

CHAPTER 1

···

A ROBUST LAYERED CONTROL SYSTEM FOR A MOBILE ROBOT

This is by far the most referenced paper that I have written. It both introduced the notion of behavior-based robotics, although that name only came much later, and described the first instance of a robot programmed in this manner. I first gave a talk on this work in Gouvieux-Chantilly, France, in late 1985. Only many years later did I learn that in the back row senior robotics people were shaking their heads asking each other why I was throwing my career away. The content of this paper was shocking because it argued for simplicity rather than for mathematical complexity of analysis and implementation. To this day many people still find the contents of this paper entirely disreputable because it is not filled with mathematical equations. Having spent six years in a mathematics department I am not afraid of mathematics, indeed I revere beautiful mathematics. But I am afraid that many people have severe cases of physics envy *and feel that their work is not complete if it does not have pages of equations, independently of whether those equations shed any light at all on the deep questions. To my mind there has to date been no decent mathematical analysis of the ideas presented in this paper and further developed by many, many researchers during the rise of behavior-based robotics. That is not to say there should not or can not be such an analysis. But I think it will require some very deep insights and can not rely on surface level equation generation.*

Abstract. We describe a new architecture for controlling mobile robots. Layers of control system are built to let the robot operate at increasing levels of competence. Layers are made up of asynchronous modules which communicate over low bandwidth channels. Each module is an instance of a fairly simple computational machine. Higher level layers can subsume the roles of lower levels by suppressing their outputs. However,

Originally appeared in the *IEEE Journal of Robotics and Automation, RA-2* April, 1986, pp. 14–23.

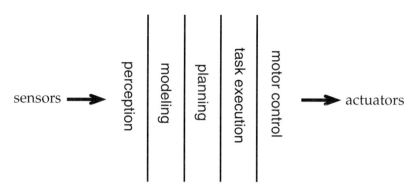

Figure 1: A traditional decomposition of a mobile robot control system into functional modules.

lower levels continue to function as higher levels are added. The result is a robust and flexible robot control system. The system has been used to control a mobile robot wandering around unconstrained laboratory areas and computer machine rooms. Eventually it is intended to control a robot that wanders the office areas of our laboratory, building maps of its surroundings using an onboard arm to perform simple tasks.

1   Introduction

A control system for a completely autonomous mobile robot must perform many complex information processing tasks in real time. It operates in an environment where the boundary conditions (viewing the instantaneous control problem in a classical control theory formulation) are changing rapidly. In fact the determination of those boundary conditions is done over very noisy channels since there is no straightforward mapping between sensors (e.g., TV cameras) and the form required of the boundary conditions.

The usual approach to building control systems for such robots is to decompose the problem into a series (roughly) of *functional units* as illustrated by a series of vertical slices in Figure 1. After analyzing the computational requirements for a mobile robot we have decided to use *task achieving behaviors* as our primary decomposition of the problem. This is illustrated by a series of horizontal slices in Figure 2. As with a functional decomposition we implement each slice explicitly then tie them all together to form a robot control system. Our new decomposition leads to a radically different architecture for mobile robot control systems, with radically different implementation strategies plausible at

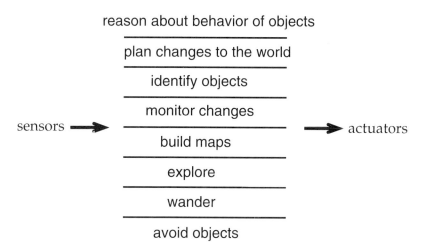

reason about behavior of objects

plan changes to the world

identify objects

monitor changes

sensors ⟶   ⟶ actuators

build maps

explore

wander

avoid objects

Figure 2: A decomposition of a mobile robot control system based on task achieving behaviors.

the hardware level, and with a large number of advantages concerning robustness, buildability and testability.

1.1   Requirements

We can identify a number of requirements of a control system for an intelligent autonomous mobile robot. They each put constraints on possible control systems we might build and employ.

Multiple Goals: Often the robot will have multiple goals, some conflicting, which it is trying to achieve. It may be trying to reach a certain point ahead of it while avoiding local obstacles. It may be trying to reach a certain place in minimal time while conserving power reserves. Often the relative importance of goals will be context dependent. Getting off the railroad tracks when a train is heard becomes much more important than inspecting the last 10 track ties of the current track section. The control system must be responsive to high priority goals, while still servicing necessary "low level" goals (e.g., in getting off the railroad tracks it is still important that the robot maintains its balance so it doesn't fall down).

Multiple Sensors: The robot will most likely have multiple sensors (e.g., TV cameras, encoders on steering and drive mechanisms, and perhaps infrared beacon detectors, an inertial navigation system, acoustic rangefinders, infrared rangefinders, access to a global positioning satellite system, etc.). All sensors have an error component in their readings.

Furthermore, often there is no direct analytic mapping from sensor values to desired physical quantities. Some of the sensors will overlap in the physical quantities they measure. They will often give inconsistent readings—sometimes due to normal sensor error and sometimes due to the measurement conditions being such that the sensor (and subsequent processing) is being used outside its domain of applicability. Often there will be no analytic characterization of the domain of applicability (e.g., under what precise conditions does the Sobel operator return valid edges?). The robot must make decisions under these conditions.

Robustness: The robot ought to be robust. When some sensors fail it should be able to adapt and cope by relying on those still functional. When the environment changes drastically it should be able to still achieve some modicum of sensible behavior, rather then sit in shock, or wander aimlessly or irrationally around. Ideally it should also continue to function well when there are faults in parts of its processor(s).

Extensibility: As more sensors and capabilities are added to a robot it needs more processing power; otherwise the original capabilities of the robot will be impaired relative to the flow of time.

1.2   Other Approaches

Multiple Goals: Elfes & Talukdar (1983) designed a control language for Moravec (1983)'s robot which tried to accommodate multiple goals. It mainly achieved this by letting the user explicitly code for parallelism and to code an exception path to a special handler for each plausible case of unexpected conditions.

Multiple Sensors: Flynn (1985) explicitly investigated the use of multiple sensors, with complementary characteristics (sonar is wide angle but reasonably accurate in depth, while infrared is very accurate in angular resolution but terrible in depth measurement). Her system has the virtue that if one sensor fails the other still delivers readings that are useful to the higher level processing. Giralt, Chatila & Vaisset (1984) use a laser range finder for map making, sonar sensors for local obstacle detection, and infrared beacons for map calibration. The robot operates in a mode where one particular sensor type is used at a time and the others are completely ignored, even though they may be functional. In the natural world multiple redundant sensors are abundant. For instance Kreithen (1983) reports that pigeons have more than four independent orientation sensing systems (e.g., sun position compared to internal biological clock). It is interesting that the sensors do not seem to be combined but rather, depending on the environmental conditions and operational level of sensor subsystems, the data from one sensor tends to dominate.

Robustness: The above work tries to make systems robust in terms of sensor availability, but little has been done with making either the behavior or the processor of a robot robust.

Extensibility: There are three ways this can be achieved without completely rebuilding the physical control system. (1) Excess processor power which was previously being wasted can be utilized. Clearly this is a bounded resource. (2) The processor(s) can be upgraded to an architecturally compatible but faster system. The original software can continue to run, but now excess capacity will be available and we can proceed as in the first case. (3) More processors can be added to carry the new load. Typically systems builders then get enmeshed in details of how to make all memory uniformly accessible to all processors. Usually the cost of the memory to processor routing system soon comes to dominate the cost (the measure of cost is not important—it can be monetary, silicon area, access time delays, or something else) of the system. As a result there is usually a fairly small upper bound (on the order of hundreds for traditional style processing units; on the order to tens to hundreds of thousands for extremely simple processors) on the number of processors which can be added.

1.3 Starting Assumptions

Our design decisions for our mobile robot are based on nine dogmatic principles (six of these principles were presented more fully in Brooks (1985)):

1. Complex (and useful) behavior need not necessarily be a product of an extremely complex control system. Rather, complex behavior may simply be the reflection of a complex environment (Simon 1969). It may be an observer who ascribes complexity to an organism—not necessarily its designer.

2. Things should be simple. This has two applications. (1) When building a system of many parts one must pay attention to the interfaces. If you notice that a particular interface is starting to rival in complexity the components it connects, then either the interface needs to be rethought or the decomposition of the system needs redoing. (2) If a particular component or collection of components solves an unstable or ill-conditioned problem, or, more radically, if its design involved the solution of an unstable or ill-conditioned problem, then it is probably not a good solution from the standpoint of robustness of the system.

3. We want to build cheap robots which can wander around human inhabited space with no human intervention, advice or control and at the same time do useful work. Map making is therefore of crucial importance even when idealized blue prints of an environment are available.

4. The human world is three dimensional; it is not just a two dimensional surface map. The robot must model the world as three dimensional if it is to be allowed to continue cohabitation with humans.

5. Absolute coordinate systems for a robot are the source of large cumulative errors. Relational maps are more useful to a mobile robot. This alters the design space for perception systems.

6. The worlds where mobile robots will do useful work are not constructed of exact simple polyhedra. While polyhedra may be useful models of a realistic world, it is a mistake to build a special world such that the models can be exact. For this reason we will build no artificial environment for our robot.

7. Sonar data, while easy to collect, does not by itself lead to rich descriptions of the world useful for truly intelligent interactions. Visual data is much better for that purpose. Sonar data may be useful for low level interactions such as real time obstacle avoidance.

8. For robustness sake the robot must be able to perform when one or more of its sensors fails or starts giving erroneous readings. Recovery should be quick. This implies that built-in self calibration must be occurring at all times. If it is good enough to achieve our goals then it will necessarily be good enough to eliminate the need for external calibration steps. To force the issue we do not incorporate any explicit calibration steps for our robot. Rather we try to make all processing steps self calibrating.

9. We are interested in building *artificial beings*—robots that can survive for days, weeks and months, without human assistance, in a dynamic complex environment. Such robots must be self sustaining.

2   Levels and Layers

There are many possible approaches to building an autonomous intelligent mobile robot. As with most engineering problems they all start by decomposing the problem into pieces, solving the subproblems for each piece, and then composing the solutions. We think we have done the first of these three steps differently to other groups. The second and third steps also differ as a consequence.

2.1   Levels of Competence

Typically mobile robot builders (e.g., (Nilsson 1984), (Moravec 1983), (Giralt et al. 1984), (Kanayama 1983), (Tsuji 1985), (Crowley 1985)) have sliced the problem into some subset of:

- sensing,

- mapping sensor data into a world representation,

- planning,

- task execution, and

- motor control.

This decomposition can be regarded as a horizontal decomposition of the problem into vertical slices. The slices form a chain through which information flows from the robot's environment, via sensing, through the robot and back to the environment, via action, closing the feedback loop (of course most implementations of the above subproblems include internal feedback loops also). An instance of each piece must be built in order to run the robot at all. Later changes to a particular piece (to improve it or extend its functionality) must either be done in such a way that the interfaces to adjacent pieces do not change, or the effects of the change must be propagated to neighboring pieces, changing their functionality too.

We have chosen instead to decompose the problem vertically as our primary way of slicing up the problem. Rather than slice the problem on the basis of internal workings of the solution we slice the problem on the basis of desired external manifestations of the robot control system.

To this end we have defined a number of *levels of competence* for an autonomous mobile robot. A level of competence is an informal specification of a desired class of behaviors for a robot over all environments it will encounter. A higher level of competence implies a more specific desired class of behaviors.

We have used the following levels of competence (an earlier version of these was reported in Brooks (1984a)) as a guide in our work:

0. Avoid contact with objects (whether the objects move or are stationary).

1. Wander aimlessly around without hitting things.

2. "Explore" the world by seeing places in the distance which look reachable and heading for them.

3. Build a map of the environment and plan routes from one place to another.

4. Notice changes in the "static" environment.

5. Reason about the world in terms of identifiable objects and perform tasks related to certain objects.

6. Formulate and execute plans which involve changing the state of the world in some desirable way.

7. Reason about the behavior of objects in the world and modify plans accordingly.

Notice that each level of competence includes as a subset each earlier level of competence. Since a level of competence defines a class of valid behaviors it can be seen that higher levels of competence provide additional constraints on that class.

2.2   Layers of Control

The key idea of levels of competence is that we can build layers of a control system corresponding to each level of competence and simply add a new layer to an existing set to move to the next higher level of overall competence.

We start by building a complete robot control system which achieves level *0* competence. It is debugged thoroughly. We never alter that system. We call it the zeroth level control system, Next we build a another control layer, which we call the first level control system. It is able to examine data from the level *0* system and is also permitted to inject data into the internal interfaces of level *0* suppressing the normal data flow. This layer, with the aid of the zeroth, achieves level *1* competence. The zeroth layer continues to run unaware of the layer above it which sometimes interferes with its data paths.

The same process is repeated to achieve higher levels of competence. See Figure 3.

We call this architecture a *subsumption architecture*.

In such a scheme we have a working control system for the robot very early in the piece—as soon as we have built the first layer. Additional layers can be added later, and the initial working system need never be changed.

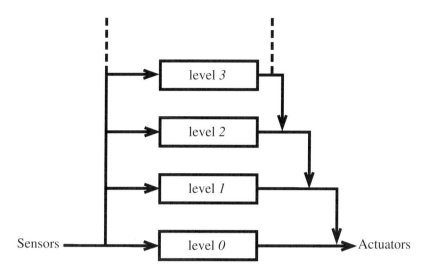

Figure 3: Control is layered with higher level layers subsuming the roles of lower level layers when they wish to take control. The system can be partitioned at any level, and the layers below form a complete operational control system.

We claim that this architecture naturally lends itself to solving the problems for mobile robots delineated in section 1.1.

Multiple Goals: Individual layers can be working on individual goals concurrently. The suppression mechanism then mediates the actions that are taken. The advantage here is that there is no need to make an early decision on which goal should be pursued. The results of pursuing all of them to some level of conclusion can be used for the ultimate decision.

Multiple Sensors: In part we can ignore the sensor fusion problem as stated earlier using a subsumption architecture. Not all sensors need to feed into a central representation. Indeed certain readings of all sensors need not feed into central representations—only those which perception processing identifies as extremely reliable might be eligible to enter such a central representation. At the same time however the sensor values may still be being used by the robot. Other layers may be processing them in some fashion and using the results to achieve their own goals, independent of how other layers may be scrutinizing them.

Robustness: Multiple sensors clearly add to the robustness of a system when their results can be used intelligently. There is another source of robustness in a subsumption architecture. Lower levels which have been well debugged continue to run when higher levels are added. Since a higher level can only suppress the outputs of lower levels by actively interfering with replacement data, in the cases that it can not produce results in a timely fashion the lower levels will still produce results which are sensible, albeit at a lower level of competence.

Extensibility: An obvious way to handle extensibility is to make each new layer run on its own processor. We will see below that this is practical as there are in general fairly low bandwidth requirements on communication channels between layers. In addition we will see that the individual layers can easily be spread over many loosely coupled processors.

2.3   The Structure of Layers

But what about building each individual layer? Don't we need to decompose a single layer in the traditional manner? This is true to some extent, but the key difference is that we don't need to account for all desired perceptions and processing and generated behaviors in a single decomposition. We are free to use different decompositions for different sensor-set task-set pairs.

We have chosen to build layers from a set of small processors which send messages to each other.

Each processor is a finite state machine with the ability to hold some data structures. Processors send messages over connecting "wires". There is no handshaking or acknowledgement of messages. The processors run completely asynchronously, monitoring their input wires, and sending messages on their output wires. It is possible for messages to get lost—it actually happens quite often. There is no other form of communication between processors, in particular there is no shared global memory.

All processors (which we refer to as modules) are created equal in the sense that within a layer there is no central control. Each module merely does its thing as best it can.

Inputs to modules can be suppressed and outputs can be inhibited by wires terminating from other modules. This is the mechanism by which higher level layers subsume the role of lower levels.

3   A Robot Control System Specification Language

There are two aspects to the components of our layered control architecture. One is the internal structure of the modules, and the second is the way in which they communicate. In this section we flesh out the details of the semantics of our modules and explain a description language for them.

3.1   Finite State Machines

Each module, or processor, is a finite state machine, augmented with some instance variables which can actually hold LISP data structures.

Each module has a number of input lines and a number of output lines. Input lines have single element buffers. The most recently arrived message is always available for inspection. Messages can be lost if a new one arrives on an input line before the last was inspected.

There is a distinguished input to each module called **reset**.

Each state is named. When the system first starts up all modules start in the distinguished state named **NIL**. When a signal is received on the reset line the module switches to state **NIL**. A state can be specified as one of four types.

Output   An output message, computed as a function of the module's input buffers and instance variables, is sent to an output line. A new specified state is then entered.

Side effect   One of the module's instance variables is set to a new value computed as a function of its input buffers and variables. A new specified state is then entered.

Conditional dispatch

A predicate on the module's instance variables and input buffers is computed and depending on the outcome one of two subsequent states is entered.

Event dispatch   An sequence of pairs of conditions and states to branch to are monitored until one of the events is true. The events are in combinations of arrivals of messages on input lines and the expiration of time delays.[1]

An example of a module defined in our specification language is the **avoid** module:

---

[1] The exact semantics are as follows. After an event dispatch is executed all input lines are monitored for message arrivals. When the next event dispatch is executed it has access to latches which indicate whether new messages arrived on each input line. Each condition is evaluated in turn. If it is true then the dispatch to the new state happens. Each condition is an and/or expression on the input line latches. In addition, condition expressions can include delay terms which become true a specified amount of time after the beginning of the execution of the event dispatch. An event dispatch waits until one of its condition expressions is true.

```
(defmodule avoid 1
  :inputs (force heading)
  :outputs (command)
  :instance-vars (resultforce)
  :states
    ((nil (event-dispatch (and force heading)
                          plan))
     (plan (setf resultforce
                 (select-direction force
                                   heading))
           go)
     (go (conditional-dispatch
           (significant-force-p resultforce
                                1.0)
          start
          nil))
     (start (output command
                    (follow-force resultforce))
            nil))))
```

Here, each of **select-direction**, **significant-force-p** and **follow-force** are LISP functions, while **setf** is the modern LISP assignment special form.

The force input line inputs a force with magnitude and direction found by treating each point found by the sonars as the site of a repulsive force decaying as the square of distance. Function **select-direction** takes this and combines it with the input on the heading line considered as a motive force. It selects the instantaneous direction of travel by summing the forces acting on the robot. (This simple technique computes the tangent to the minimum energy path computed by Khatib (1983).)

Function **significant-force-p** checks whether the resulting force is above some threshold—in this case it determines whether the resulting motion would take less than a second. The dispatch logic then ignores such motions.

Function **follow-force** converts the desired direction and force magnitude into motor velocity commands.

This particular module is part of the level *1* (as indicated by the argument "1" following the name of the module) control system described below. It essentially does local navigation, making sure obstacles are avoided by diverting a desired heading away from obstacles. It does not deliver the robot to a desired location—that is the task of level *2* competence.

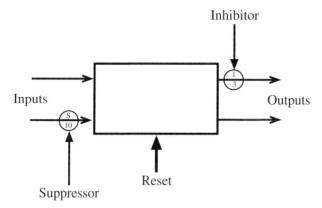

Figure 4: A module has input and output lines. Input signals can be suppressed and replaced with the suppressing signal. Output signals can be inhibited. A module can also be reset to state NIL.

3.2   Communication

Figure 4 shows the best way to think about these finite state modules for the purposes of communications. They have some input lines and some output lines. An output line from one module is connected to input lines of one or more other modules. One can think of these lines as wires, each with sources and a destination.

Additionally outputs may be inhibited, and inputs may be suppressed.

An extra wire can terminate (i.e., have its destination) at an output site of a module. If *any* signal travels along this wire it *inhibits* any output message from the module along that line for some pre-determined time. Any messages sent by the module to that output during that time period is lost.

Similarly an extra wire can terminate at an input site of a module. Its action is very similar to that of inhibition, but additionally, the signal on this wire, besides inhibiting signals along the usual path, actually gets fed through as the input to the module. Thus it *suppresses* the usual input and provides a replacement. If more than one suppressing wire is present they are essentially 'or'-ed together.

For both suppression and inhibition we write the time constants inside the circle.

In our specification language we write wires as a source (i.e., an output line) followed by a number of destinations (i.e., input lines). For instance the connection to the force input of the **avoid** module defined above might be the wire defined as:

```
(defwire 1 (feelforce force) (avoid force))
```

This links the force output of the **feelforce** module to the input of the **avoid** module in the level one control system.

Suppression and inhibition can also be described with a small extension to the syntax above. Below we see the suppression of the command input of the **turn** module, a level *0* module by a signal from the level *1* module **avoid**.

```
(defwire 1 (avoid command)
          ((suppress (turn command) 20.0)))
```

In a similar manner a signal can be connected to the reset input of a module.

4   A Robot Control System Instance

We have implemented a mobile robot control system to achieve levels *0* and *1* competence as defined above, and have started implementation of level *2* bringing it to a stage which exercises the fundamental subsumption idea effectively. We need more work on an early vision algorithm to complete level *2*.

4.1   Zeroth Level

The lowest level layer of control makes sure that the robot does not come into contact with other objects. It thus achieves level *0* competence. See Figure 5. If something approaches the robot it will move away. If in the course of moving itself it is about to collide with an object it will halt. Together these two tactics are sufficient for the robot to flee from moving obstacles, perhaps requiring many motions, without colliding with stationary obstacles. The combination of the tactics allows the robot to operate with with very coarsely calibrated sonars and a wide range of repulsive force functions. Theoretically, the robot is not invincible of course, and a sufficiently fast moving object, or a very cluttered environment might result in a collision. Over the course of a number of hours of autonomous operation, our physical robot (see section 5.2) has not collided with either a moving or fixed obstacle. The moving obstacles have, however, been careful to move slowly.

- The **turn** and **forward** modules communicate with the actual robot. They have extra communication mechanisms, allowing

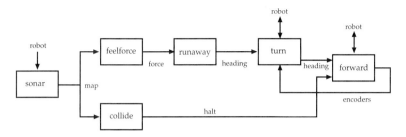

Figure 5: The level *0* control system.

them to send and receive commands to and from the physical robot directly. The **turn** module receives a heading specifying an inplace turn angle followed by a forward motion of a specified magnitude. It commands the robot to turn (and at the same time sends a busy message on an additional output channel illustrate in Figure 7) and on completion passes on the heading to the **forward** module (and also reports the shaft encoder readings on another output line shown in Figure 7) then goes into a wait state ignoring all incoming messages. The **forward** module commands the robot to move forward, but halts it if it receives and message on its halt input line during the motion. As soon as the robot is idle its sends out the shaft encoder readings–the message acts as a reset for the **turn** module, which is then once again ready to accept a new motion command. Notice the any heading commands sent to the **turn** module during transit are lost.

- The **sonar** module takes a vector of sonar readings, filters them for invalid readings, and effectively produces a robot centered map of obstacles in polar coordinates.

- The **collide** module monitors the sonar map and if it detects objects dead ahead it sends a signal on the halt line to the **motor** module. The **collide** module does not know or care whether the robot is moving. Halt messages sent while the robot is stationary are essentially lost.

- The **feelforce** module sums the results of considering each detected object as a repulsive force, generating a single resultant force.

- The **runaway** module monitors the 'force' produced by the sonar detected obstacles and sends commands to the **turn** module if it ever becomes significant.

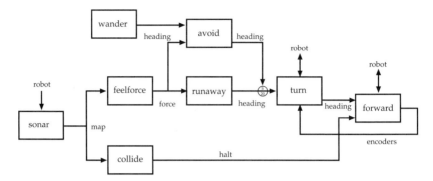

Figure 6: The level *0* control system augmented with the level *1* system.

Figure 5 gives a complete description of how the modules are connected together.

4.2   First Level

The first level layer of control, when combined with the zeroth, imbues the robot with the ability to wander around aimlessly without hitting obstacles. This was defined earlier as level *1* competence. This control level relies in a large degree on the zeroth level's aversion to hitting obstacles. In addition it uses a simple heuristic to plan ahead a little in order to avoid potential collisions which would need to be handled by the zeroth level.

- The **wander** module generates a new heading for the robot every 10 seconds or so.

- The **avoid** module, described in more detail in section 3, takes the result of the force computation from the zeroth level, and combines it with the desired heading to produce a modified heading which usually points in roughly the right direction, but is perturbed to avoid any obvious obstacles. This computation implicitly subsumes the computations of the **runaway** module, in the case that there is also a heading to consider. In fact the output of the **avoid** module suppresses the output from the **runaway** module as it enters the **motor** module.

Figure 6 gives a complete description of how the modules are connected together. Note that it is simply Figure 5 with some more modules and wires added.

4.3 Second Level

Level two is meant to add an exploratory mode of behavior to the robot, using visual observations to select interesting places to visit. A vision module finds corridors of free space. Additional modules provide a means of position servoing the robot to along the corridor despite the presence of local obstacles on its path (as detected with the sonar sensing system). The wiring diagram is shown in Figure 7. Note that it is simply Figure 6 with some more modules and wires added.

- The **status** module monitors the **turn** and **forward** modules. It maintains one status output which sends either *hi* or *lo* messages to indicate whether the robot is busy. In addition, at the completion of every turn and roll forward combination it sends out a combined set of shaft encoder readings.

- The **whenlook** module monitors the busy line from the **status** module, and whenever the robot has been sitting idle for a few seconds it decides its time to look for a corridor to traverse. It inhibits wandering so it can take some pictures and process them without wandering away from its current location, and resets the **pathplan** and **integrate** modules–this latter action ensures that it will know how far it has moved from its observation point should any **runaway** impulses perturb it.

- The **look** module initiates the vision processing, and waits for a candidate freeway. It filters out poor candidates and passes any acceptable one to the **pathplan** module.

- The **stereo** module is supposed to use stereo TV images (Grimson 1985), obtained by the robot, to find a corridor of free space. At the time of writing final version of this module had not been implemented. Instead, both in simulation and on the physical robot, we have replaced it with a sonar-base corridor finder.

- The **integrate** module accumulates reports of motions from the **status** module and always sends its most recent result out on its integral line. It gets restarted by application of a signal to its reset input.

- The **pathplan** module takes a goal specification (in terms of an angle to turn, a distance to travel) and attempts to reach that goal. To do this it sends headings to the **avoid** module, which may perturb them to avoid local obstacles, and monitors its integral input which is an integration of actual motions. The messages to

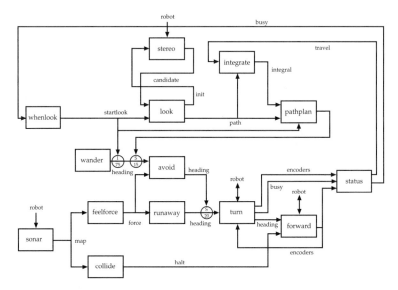

Figure 7: The level *0* and *1* control systems augmented with the level *2* system.

the **avoid** module suppress random wanderings of the robot, so long as the higher level planner remains active. When the position of the robot is close to the desired position (the robot is unaware of control errors due to wheel slippage etc., so this is a dead reckoning decision) it terminates.

The current wiring of the second level of control is shown in Figure 7, augmenting the two lower level control systems. The zeroth and first layers still play an active role during normal operation of the second layer.

5   Performance

The control system described here has been used extensively to control both a simulated robot and an actual physical robot wandering around a cluttered laboratory and a machine room.

5.1   A Simulated Robot

The simulation tries to simulate all the errors and uncertainties that exist in the world of the real robot. When commanded to turn through angle α and travel distance d the simulated robot actually turns through

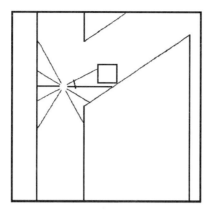

Figure 8: The simulated robot receives 12 sonar readings. Some sonar beams glance off walls and do not return within a certain time.

---

angle $\alpha + \delta\alpha$ and travels distance $d + \delta d$. Its sonars can bounce off walls multiple times, and even when they do return they have a noise component in the readings modeling thermal and humidity effects. We feel it is important to have such a realistic simulation. Anything less leads to incorrect control algorithms.

The simulator runs off a clock and runs at the same rate as would the actual robot. It actually runs on the same processor that is simulating the subsumption architecture. Together they are nevertheless able to perform a realtime simulation of the robot and its control and also drive graphics displays of robot state and module performance monitors. Figure 8 shows the robot (which itself is not drawn) receiving sonar reflections at some of its 12 sensors. Other beams did not return within the time allocated for data collection. The beams are being reflected by various walls. There is a small bar in front of the robot perpendicular to the direction the robot is pointing.

Figure 9 shows an example world in two dimensional projection. The simulated robot with a first level control system connected was allowed to wander from an initial position. The squiggly line traces out its path. Note that it was wandering aimlessly and that it hit no obstacles.

Figure 10 shows two examples of the same scene and the motion of the robot with the second level control system connected. In these cases the **stereo** module was supplanted with a situation specific module which gave out two precise corridor descriptions. While achieving the goals of following these corridors the lower level wandering behavior was suppressed. However the obstacle avoiding behavior of the lower

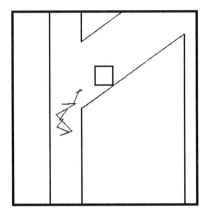

Figure 9: Under levels *0* and *1* control the robot wanders around aimlessly. It does not hit obstacles.

---

levels continued to function–in both cases the robot avoided the square obstacle. The goals were not reached exactly. The simulator models a uniformly distributed error of $\pm 5\%$ in both turn and forward motion. As soon as the goals had been achieved satisfactorily the robot reverted to its wandering behavior.

5.2   A Physical Robot

We have constructed a mobile robot shown in Figure 11. It is about 17 inches in diameter and about 30 inches from the ground to the top platform. Most of the processing occurs offboard on a LISP MACHINE.

The drive mechanism was purchased from Real World Interface of Sudbury, Massachusetts. Three parallel drive wheels are steered together. The two motors are servoed by a single microprocessor. The robot body is attached to the steering mechanism and always points in the same direction as the wheels. It can turn in place (actually it inscribes a circle about 1 cm in diameter).

Currently installed sensors are a ring of twelve Polaroid sonar time of flight range sensors and two Sony CCD cameras. The sonars are arranged symmetrically around the rotating body of the robot. The cameras are on a tilt head (pan is provided by the steering motors). We plan to install feelers which can sense objects at ground level about six inches from the base extremities.

A central cardcage contains the main onboard processor, an Intel 8031. It communicates with offboard processors via a 12Kbit/sec du-

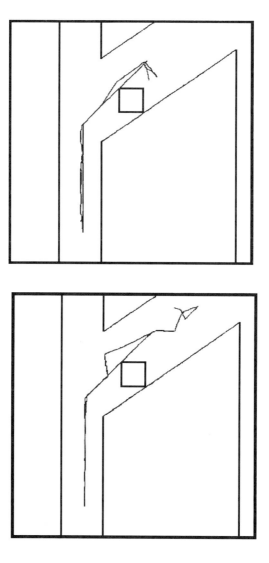

Figure 10: With level *2* control the robot tries to achieve commanded goals. The nominal goals are the two straight lines. After reaching the second goal, since there are no new goals forthcoming, the robot reverts to aimless level *1* behavior.

Figure 11: The MIT AI Lab mobile robot.

plex radio link. The radios are modified Motorola digital voice encryption units. Error correction cuts the effective bit rate to less than half the nominal rating. The 8031 passes commands down to the motor controller processor and returns encoder readings. It controls the sonars, and the tilt head and switches the cameras through a single channel video transmitter mounted on top of the robot. The latter transmits a standard TV signal to a LISP MACHINE equipped with a demodulator and frame grabber.

The robot has spent a few hours wandering around a laboratory and a machine room.

Under level *0* control the robot finds a large empty space and then sits there contented until a moving obstacle approaches. Two people together can successfully herd the robot just about anywhere–through doors or between rows of disk drives, for instance.

When level *1* control is added the robot is no longer content to sit in an open space. After a few seconds it heads off in a random direction. Our uncalibrated sonars and obstacle repulsion functions make it overshoot a little to locations where the **runaway** module reacts. It would be interesting to make this the basis of adaption of certain parameters.

Under level *2* a sonar-based corridor finder usually finds the most distant point in the room. The robot heads of in the direction. People walking in front of the robot cause it to detour, but still get to the initially desired goal even when it involves squeezing between closely spaced obstacles. If the sonars are in error and a goal is selected beyond a wall, say, the robot usually ends up in a position where the attractive force of the goal is within a threshold used by **avoid** of the repulsive forces of the wall. At this point **avoid** does not issue any heading, as it would be for some trivial motion of the robot. The robot sits still defeated by the obstacle. The **whenlook** module, however, notices that the robot is idle and initiates a new scan for another corridor of free space to follow.

5.3 Implementation Issues

While we have been able to simulate sufficient processors on a single LISP MACHINE up until now, that capability will soon pass as we bring on line our vision work (the algorithms have been debugged as traditional serial algorithms but we plan on re-implementing them within the subsumption architecture). Building the architecture in custom chips is a long term goal.

One of the motivations for developing the layered control system was extensibility of processing power. The fact that it is decomposed into asynchronous processors with low bandwidth communication and no shared memory should certainly assist in achieving that goal. New processors can simply be added to the network by connecting their inputs and outputs at appropriate places—there are no bandwidth or synchronization considerations in such connections.

The finite state processors need not be large. Sixteen states is more than sufficient for all modules we have so far written. (Actually 8 states are sufficient under the model of the processors we have presented here and used in our simulations. However we have refined the design somewhat towards gate level implementation and there we use simpler more numerous states.) Many such processors could easily be packed on a single chip.

The LISP programs that are called by the finite state machines are all rather simple. We believe it is possible to implement each of them with a simple network of comparators, selectors, polar coordinate vector adders and monotonic function generators. The silicon area overhead for each module would probably not be larger than that required for the finite state machine itself.

6   Conclusion

The key ideas in this paper are:

- The mobile robot control problem can be decomposed in terms of behaviors rather than in terms of functional modules.

- It provides a way to incrementally build and test a complex mobile robot control system.

- Useful parallel computation can be performed on a low bandwidth loosely coupled network of asynchronous simple processors. The topology of that network is relatively fixed.

- There is no need for a central control module of a mobile robot. The control system can be viewed as a system of agents each busy with their own solipsist world.

Besides leading to a different implementation strategy it is also interesting to note the way the decomposition affected the capabilities of the robot control system we have built. In particular our control system deals with moving objects in the environment at the very lowest level, and has a specific module (**runaway**) for that purpose. Traditionally mobile robot projects have delayed handling moving objects in the environment beyond the scientific life of the project.
Note: A drawback of the presentation in this paper was a merging of the algorithms for control of the robot from the implementation medium. We felt this was necessary to convince the reader of the utility of both. It is unlikely that the subsumption architecture would appear to be useful without a clear demonstration of how a respectable and useful algorithm can run on it. Mixing the two descriptions as we have done demonstrates the proposition.

7   Acknowledgements

Tomás Lozano-Pérez, Eric Grimson, Jon Connell and Anita Flynn have all provided helpful comments on earlier drafts of this paper.
    This work was supported in part by an IBM Faculty Development Award, in part by a grant from the Systems Development Foundation, in part by an equipment grant from Motorola, and in part by the Advanced Research Projects Agency under Office of Naval Research contracts N00014–80–C–0505 and N00014–82–K–0334.

CHAPTER 2

···
A ROBOT THAT WALKS: EMERGENT BEHAVIORS FROM
A CAREFULLY EVOLVED NETWORK

After building the robot described in the previous paper we were quickly able to construct a number of similar robots, all with wheels, but of varying sizes and with varying physical implementations of the subsumption architecture. *But through 1988 most of these robots simply wandered around doing some search task or another, and avoided obstacles, or chased other robots. Early in 1988 the thought occured that we should be able to get the robots to do something more. A walking robot seemed an interesting idea, but since a colleague was working in the same building on one, two, and four-legged robots it seemed appropriate that I try a six-legged robot. There had been only a couple of previous six-legged robots and they required immensely complex control systems. Thus they seemed a good challenge for the subsumption architecture. Additionally, by making the robot much smaller than others had tried we made a lot of the control problems much simpler. So Grinnell More, Colin Angle, and I worked for twelve weeks over the summer of 1988 to develop Genghis. At no point did we intentionally make the robot insect-like in its appearance, but it certainly ended up that way. Our belief was that it was a case of convergent evolution to an optimal layout once the basic body pattern of bilaterally symmetric pairs of three legs organized in a linear fashion was chosen. I built a completely new implementation of the subsumption architecture to run on an 8-bit processor and a separate operating system to run on the 2 actuator and 1 sensor processors on board the 30cm long robot. It was the best academic summer of my life. The development of the actual walking code, the subject of this paper, once the new compiler and low level network code was in place, took only about 10 days. It confirmed in my mind that we were really on to something significant with the behavior-based approach to robotics. Genghis now resides in the Smithsonian Air and Space Museum.*

Originally appeared in *Neural Computation, 1:2,* Summer 1989, pp. 253–262.

Abstract. Most animals have significant behavioral expertise built in without having to explicitly learn it all from scratch. This expertise is a product of evolution of the organism; it can be viewed as a very long term form of learning which provides a structured system within which individuals might learn more specialized skills or abilities. This paper suggests one possible mechanism for analagous robot evolution by describing a carefully designed series of networks, each one being a strict augmentation of the previous one, which control a six-legged walking machine capable of walking over rough terrain and following a person passively sensed in the infrared spectrum. As the completely decentralized networks are augmented, the robot's performance and behavior repetoire demonstrably improve. The rationale for such demonstrations is that they may provide a hint as to the requirements for automatically building massive networks to carry out complex sensory-motor tasks. The experiments with an actual robot ensure that an essence of reality is maintained and that no critical disabling problems have been ignored.

1   Introduction

In earlier work, (Brooks 1986), (Brooks & Connell 1986), we have demonstrated complex control systems for mobile robots built from completely distributed networks of augmented finite state machines. In this paper we demonstrate that these techniques can be used to incrementally build complex systems integrating relatively large numbers of sensory inputs and large numbers of actuator outputs. Each step in the construction is purely incremental, but nevertheless along the way viable control systems are left at each step, before the next little piece of network is added. Additionally we demonstrate how complex behaviors, such as walking, can emerge from a network of rather simple reflexes with little central control. This contradicts vague hypotheses made to the contrary during the study of insect walking (e.g., Bassler (1983), page 112).

2   The Subsumption Architecture

The subsumption architecture (Brooks 1986) provides an incremental method for building robot control systems linking perception to action. A properly designed network of finite state machines, augmented with internal timers, provides a robot with a certain level of performance, and a repetoire of behaviors. The architecture provides mechanisms to augment such networks in a purely incremental way to improve the robot's performance on tasks and to increase the range of tasks it can perform. At an architectural level, the robot's control system is expressed as a series of layers, each specifying a behavior pattern for the robot, and each implemented as a network of message passing augmented finite state machines. The network can be thought of as an explicit wiring diagram connected outputs of some machines to inputs of others with wires that can transmit messages. In the implementation of the architecture on the walking robot the messages are limited to 8 bits.

Each augmented finite state machine (AFSM), Figure 1, has a set of registers and a set of timers, or alarm clocks, connected to a conventional finite state machine which can control a combinatorial network fed by the registers. Registers can be written by attaching input wires to them and sending messages from other machines. The messages get written into them replacing any existing contents. The arrival of a message, or the expiration of a timer, can trigger a change of state in the interior finite state machine. Finite state machine states can either wait on some event, conditionally dispatch to one of two other states based on some combinatiorial predicate on the registers, or compute a combinatorial function of the registers directing the result either back to one of the registers or to an output of the augmented finite state machine. Some AFSMs connect directly to robot hardware. Sensors deposit their values to certain registers, and certain outputs direct commands to actuators.

A series of layers of such machines can be augmented by adding new machines and connecting them into the existing network in the ways shown in Figure 1. New inputs can be connected to existing registers, which might previously have contained a constant. New machines can inhibit existing outputs or suppress existing inputs, by being attached as side-taps to existing wires (Figure 1, circled 'i'). When a message arrives on an inhibitory side-tap no messages can travel along the existing wire for some short time period. To maintain inhibition there must be a continuous flow of messages along the new wire. (In previous versions of the subsumption architecture (Brooks 1986) explicit, long, time periods had to be specified for inhibition or suppression with single shot messages. Recent work has suggested this better approach (Connell 1988).) When a message arrives on a suppressing side-tap (Figure 1, circled 's'), again no messages are allowed to flow from the original source for some small time period, but now the suppressing message is gated through and it masquerades as having come from the original source. Again, a continous supply of suppressing messages is required to maintain control of a side-tapped wire. One last mechanism for merging two wires is called defaulting (indicated in wiring diagrams by a circled 'd'). This is just like the suppression case, except that the original wire, rather than the new side-tapping wire, is able to wrest control of messages sent to the destination.

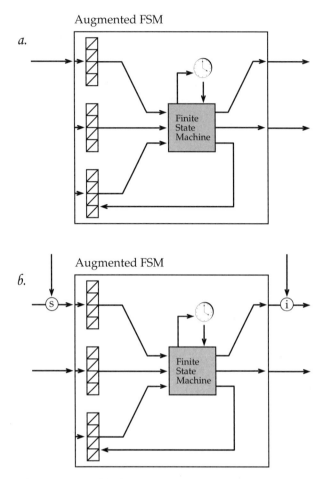

Figure 1: An augmented finite state machine consists of registers, alarm clocks, a combinatorial network and a regular finite state machine. Input messages are delivered to registers, and messages can be generated on output wires. AFSMs are wired together in networks of message passing wires. As new wires are added to a network, they can be connected to existing registers, they can inhibit outputs and they can suppress inputs.

All clocks in a subsumption system have approximately the same tick period (0.04 seconds on the walking robot), but neither they nor messages are synchronous. The fastest possible rate of sending messages along a wire is one per clock tick. The time periods used for both inibition and suppression are two clock ticks. Thus, a side-tapping wire

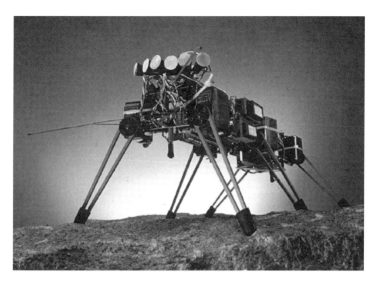

Figure 2: The six-legged robot is about 35cm long, has a leg span of 25cm, and weighs approximately 1Kg. Each leg is rigid and is attached at a shoulder joint with two degrees of rotational freedom, driven by two orthoganally mounted model airplane position controllable servo motors. An error signal has been tapped from the internal servo circuitry to provide crude force measurement (5 bits, including sign) on each axis, when the leg is not in motion around that axis. Other sensors are two front whiskers, two four-bit inclinometers (pitch and roll), and six forward looking passive pyroelectric infrared sensors. The sensors have approximately 6 degrees angular resolution and are arranged over a 45 degree span. There are four onboard 8-bit microprocessors linked by a 62.5Kbaud token ring. The total memory usage of the robot is about 1Kbytes of RAM and 10Kbytes of EPROM. Three silver-zinc batteries fit between the legs to make the robot totally self contained.

---

with messages being sent at the maximum rate can maintain control of its host wire.

3   The Networks and Emergent Behaviors

The six-legged robot is shown in Figure 2. We refer to the motors on each leg as an α motor (for *advance*) which swings the leg back and forth, and a β motor (for *balance*) which lifts the leg up and down.

Figure 3 shows a network of 57 augmented finite state machines which was built incrementally and can be run incrementally by selec-

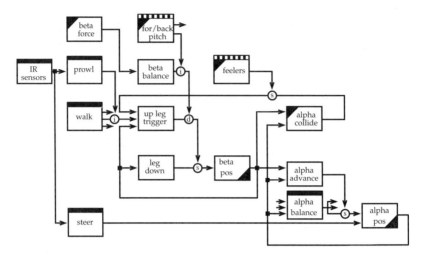

Figure 3: The final network consists of 57 augmented finite state machines. The AFSMs without bands on top are repeated six times, once for each leg. The ASFMs with solid bands are unique and comprise the only central control in making the robot walk, steer and follow targets. The AFSMs with striped bands are duplicated twice each and are specific to particular legs. The ASFMs with a filled triangle in their bottom right corner control actuators. Those with a filled triangle in their upper left corner receive inputs from sensors.

tively deactivating later AFSMs. The AFSMs without bands on top are repeated six times, once for each leg. The ASFMs with solid bands are unique and comprise the only central control in making the robot walk, steer and follow targets. The ASFMs with striped bands are duplicated twice each and are specific to particular legs.

The complete network can be built incrementally by adding AFSMs to an existing network producing a number of viable robot control systems itemized below. All additions are strictly additive with no need to change any existing structure. Figure 4 shows a partially constructed version of the network.

1 **Standup.** The simplest level of competence for the robot is achieved with just two AFSMs per leg, *alpha pos* and *beta pos*. These two machines use a register to hold a set position for the α and β motors respectively and ensure that the motors are sent those positions. The initial values for the registers are such that on power up the robot assumes a stance position. The AFSMs also provide an output that reports the most recent commanded position for their motor.

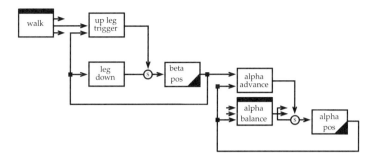

Figure 4: A strict subset of the full network enables the robot to walk without any feedback. It pitches and rolls significantly as it walks over rough terrain. This version of the network contains 32 AFSMs. 30 of these comprise six identical copies, one for each leg, of a network of five AFSMs which are purely local in their interactions with a leg. The last two machines provide all the global coordination necessary to make the machine walk; one tries to drive the sum of leg swing angles (α angles) to zero, and the other sequences lifting of individual legs.

2 **Simple walk.** A number of simple increments to this network result in one which lets the robot walk. First, a *leg down* machine for each leg is added which notices whenever the leg is not in the down position and writes the appropriate *beta pos* register in order to set the leg down. Then, a single *alpha balance* machine is added which monitors the α position, or forward swing of all six legs, treating straight out as zero, forward as positive and backward as negative. It sums these six values and sends out a single identical message to all six *alpha pos* machines, which, depending on the sign of the sum is either null, or an increment or decrement to the current α position of each leg. The *alpha balance* machine samples the leg positions at a relatively high rate. Thus if one leg happens to move forward for some reason, all legs will receive a series of messages to move backward slightly.

Next, the *alpha advance* ASFM is added for each leg. Whenever it notices that the leg is raised (by monitoring the output of the *beta pos* machine) it forces the leg forward by suppressing the signal coming from the global *alpha balance* machine. Thus, if a leg is raised for some reason it reflexively swings forward, and all other legs swing backward slightly to compensate (notice that the forward swinging leg does not even receive the backward message due to the suppression of that signal). Now a fifth ASFM, *up leg trigger* is added for each leg which can issue a command to lift a leg by suppressing the commands from the *leg down* machine. It has one register which monitors the current β position of the leg. When it is down, and a trigger message is received in a second register, it ensures that the contents of an initially constant third register, are sent to the *beta pos* machine to lift the leg.

With this combination of local leg specific machines and a single machine trying to globally coordinate the sum of the α position of all legs, the robot can very nearly walk. If an *up leg trigger* machine receives a trigger message it lifts its associated leg, which triggers a reflex to swing it foward, and then the appropriate *leg down* machine will pull the leg down. At the same time all the other legs still on the ground (those not busy moving forward) will swing backwards, moving the robot fowards.

The final piece of the puzzle is to add a single AFSM which sequences walking by sending trigger messages in some appropriate pattern to each of the six *up leg trigger* machines. We have used two versions of this machine, both of which complete a gait cycle once every 2.4 seconds. One machine produces the well known alternating tripod (Wilson 1966), by sending simultaneous lift triggers to triples of legs every 1.2 seconds. The other produces the standard back to front ripple gait by sending a trigger message to a different leg every 0.4 seconds. Other gaits are possible by simple substitution of this machine. The machine walks with this network, but is insensitive to the terrain over which it is walking and tends to roll and pitch excessively as it walks over obstacles. The complete network for this simple type of walking is shown in Figure 4.

3 **Force balancing.** A simple minded way to compenstate for rough terrain is to monitor the force on each leg as it is placed on the ground and back off if it rises beyond some threshold. The rationale is that if a leg is being placed down on an obstacle it will have to roll (or pitch) the body of the robot in order for the leg β angle to reach its preset value, increasing the load on the motor. For each leg a *beta force* machine is added which monitors the β motor forces, discarding high readings coming from servo errors during free space swinging, and a *beta balance* machine which sends out lift up messages whenever the force is too high. It includes a small deadband where it sends out zero move messages which trickle down through a defaulting switch on the *up leg trigger* to eventually suppress the *leg down* reflex. This is a form of active compliance which has a number of known problems on walking machines (Klein, Olson & Pugh 1983). On a standard obstacle course (a single 5 centimeter high obstacle on a plane) this new machine reduced the standard deviation, over a 12 second period, of the readings from onboard 4 bit pitch and roll inclinometers (with approximately a 35 degree range), from 3.592 and 0.624 respectively to 2.325 and 0.451 respectively.

4 **Leg lifting.** There is a tradeoff between how high each leg is lifted and overall walking speed. But low leg lifts limit the height of obstacles which can be easily scaled. An eighth AFSM for each leg compensates for this by measuring the force on the forward swing (α) motor as it swings forward and writing the height register in the *up leg trigger* at a higher value setting up for a higher lift of the leg on the next step cycle of that leg. The *up leg trigger* resets this value after the next step.

5 **Whiskers.** In order to anticipate obstacles better, rather than waiting until the front legs are rammed against them, each of two whiskers is monitored by a *feeler* machine and the lift of the the left and right fron legs is appropriately upped for the next step cycle.

6 **Pitch stabilization.** The simple force balancing strategy above is by no means perfect. In particular in high pitch situations the rear or front legs (depending on the direction of pitch) are heavily loaded and so tend to be lifted slightly causing the robot to sag and increase the pitch even more. Therefore one *forward pitch* and one *backward pitch* AFSM are added to monitor high pitch conditions on the pitch inclinometer and to inhibit the local *beta balance* machine output in the appropriate circumstances. The pitch standard deviation over the 12 second test reduces to 1.921 with this improvement while the roll standard deviation stays around the same at 0.458.

7 **Prowling.** Two additional AFSMs can be added so that the robot only bothers to walk when there is something moving nearby. The *IR sensors* machine monitors an array of six forward looking pyro-electric infrared sensors and sends an activity message to the *prowl* machine when it detects motion. The *prowl* machine usually inhibits the leg lifting trigger messages from the *walk* machine except for a little while after infrared activity is noticed. Thus the robot sits still until a person, say, walks by, and then it moves forward a little.

8 **Steered prowling.** The single *steer* AFSM takes note of the predominant direction, if any, of the infrared activity and writes into a register in each *alpha pos* machine for legs on that side of the robot, specifying the rear swinging stop position of the leg. This gets reset on every stepping cycle of the leg, so the *steer* machine must constantly refresh it in order to reduce the leg's backswing and force the robot to turn in the direction of the activity. With this single additional machine the robot is able to follow moving objects such as a slow walking person.

4   Conclusion

This exercise in synthetic neuro-ethology has successfully demonstrated a number of things, at least in the robot domain. All these demonstrations depend on the manner in which the networks were built incrementally from augmented finite state machines.

- Robust walking behaviors can be produced by a distributed system with very limited central coordination. In particular much of the sensory-motor integration which goes on can happen within local asynchronous units. This has relevance, in the form of an existence proof, to the debate on the central versus peripheral control of motion (Bizzi 1980) and in particular in the domain of insect walking (Bassler 1983).

- Higher level behaviors (such as following people) can be integrated into a system which controls lower level behaviors, such as leg lifting and force balancing, in a completely seamless way. There is no need to postulate qualitatively different sorts of structures for different levels of behaviors and no need to postulate unique forms of network interconnect to integrate higher level behaviors.

- Coherent macro behaviors can arise from many independent micro behaviors. For instance, the robot following people works even though most of the effort is being done by independent circuits driving legs, and these circuits are getting only very indirect pieces of information from the higher levels, and none of this communication refers at all to the task in hand (or foot).

- There is no need to postulate a central repository for sensor fusion to feed into. Conflict resolution tends to happen more at the motor command level, rather than the sensor or perception level.

Acknowledgements

Grinnell More did most of the mechanical design and fabrication of the robot. Colin Angle did much of the processor design and most of the electrical fabrication of the robot. Mike Ciholas, Jon Connell, Anita Flynn, Chris Foley and Peter Ning provided valuable design and fabrication advice and help.

This report describes research done at the Artificial Intelligence Laboratory of the Massachusetts Institute of Technology. Support for the research is provieded in part by the University Research Initiative under Office of Naval Research contract N00014–86–K–0685 and in part by the Advanced Research Projects Agency under Office of Naval Research contract N00014–85–K–0124.

CHAPTER 3

LEARNING A DISTRIBUTED MAP REPRESENTATION BASED ON NAVIGATION BEHAVIORS

Maja J. Mataric and Rodney A. Brooks

Even with Genghis the subsumption architecture *had only allowed robots to move around in an entirely reactive way, unaware of the passage of time, or of anything that had happened to them in the past. Many people saw this as a hallmark of the behavior-based approach and were extremely critical of it on that basis. The robot,* Toto, *described in this paper was a demonstration of the integration of something which was considered by many to be impossible within the behavior-based approach. Toto showed that behavior-based robots could have dynamically changeable long-term goals, and could act as if they were generating plans, and as if they built up maps over time. Toto, the MS thesis work of Maja Mataric, did all this within the framework of a completely distributed network of simple machines. There was no central controller, nor any manipulable data structure representing the map. Rather the maps that Toto built were distributed throughout the network of simple machines, and the elements which represented pieces of space were also the control elements which told the robot what to do, and how to solve planning problems when in that location in space. Furthermore the apparent plans of Toto were never existant as complete data structures. Rather they unfolded during the interaction of the robot and the environment. But to say there were no plans was incorrect. They just were not represented in the central manipulable way that computer scientists over the last forty years have come to think of as the only way to represent things. This paper is very confusing to many people. It turns the whole notion of representation upside down. The robot never has things circumscribed in its head, but it acts just like we imagine it ought to. I view this work as the nail in the coffin of traditional representationalism.*

Originally appeared in the *Proceedings of the 1990 USA-Japan Symposium on Flexible Automation* held in Kyoto, Japan, June, pp. 499–506.

1 Introduction

In this paper we describe an implemented mobile robot, Toto, which successfully builds maps and uses them to navigate. The approach is unique in that the map representation is totally distributed, using no central resources. Goal-directed computation is also completely distributed over the landmarks constituting the map.

Toto is a fully autonomous sonar-based mobile robot with an onboard 68000 microprocessor and a flux-gate compass. It uses low level competences to navigate safely in unaltered laboratory/office environments. Its competence repertoire is built through incremental integration of new behaviors. The addition of behaviors which monitor what the robot does and what its sensors measure allows for dynamic landmark detection. Rather than declaratively, the landmarks are defined procedurally as couplings of sensory readings and actions.

Landmark detection enables passive map building through wandering and observation. As the robot explores its environment, individual behaviors come to represent particular parts of the world, or landmarks.

As more behaviors are added the robot is able to make use of its map to plan and execute shortest paths appropriate for the given task. Incremental behaviors can be added to improve the robot's ability to construct and use the map.

This work can be viewed as an experiment in representation space. It is quite extreme in that we deliberately ignore information available from odometry, in order to experiment with what can be achieved with qualitative maps. It is quite extreme in that there is no central data structure at all; it is totally distributed. It is quite extreme in that map making and map use is constructed from an incremental set of layers of behaviors in such a way that the system works with some particular level of performance wherever that construction is cut off. It is quite extreme in that there is no reasoning engine separate from the map; the map is the reasoning system, specialized for the particular set of experiences encountered by the map making systems.

2 Philosophy

We believe that the way in which a problem is decomposed imposes fundamental constraints on the way in which people attempt to solve that problem. In particular, mobile robotics, and AI in general, has, since the days of Shakey (Nilsson 1984), assumed that there is a perception system which feeds into a central declarative world model, and a planning system which acts upon that world model. The MIT mobile robot group has rejected that decomposition for a number of years.

Instead (Brooks 1986), we view the fundamental decomposition as being directed by competences, each one of which may involve perception, modeling, and choosing a course of actions. The organizing principle we use is called the *subsumption architecture.*

A subsumption program is built on a computational substrate that is organized into a series of incremental layers, each, in the general case, connecting perception to action. In our case the substrate is networks of finite state machines augmented with timing elements. Each layer can assume the existence of a lower level layer, but it does not hierarchically call the lower levels as subroutines. Rather, it coexists with them, operating in an environment which consists of the both the world and the lower levels.

Subsumption programs do not in general contain a central representation of the external world. Aspects of that world appear in many places in many layers of the program. But they are then connected to action, rather than being fused into a single representation.

Subsumption programs have very successfully used the idea of distributed control. Indeed the complexity of the tasks carried out by our robots (e.g., (Connell 1989)) is often surprising given the simplicity of the underlying control programs. We believe that it is the distributed nature of our control, in contrast to a hierarchical control system, that leads to such elegant decompositions into simple and clean components.

In extending our robots to be able to deal with map making and path planning we were interested in exploring two questions:

- Could our decentralized control methodology incorporate such a thing as a map, usually thought of as a central resource, without compromising the elegance of incremental layering?

- Could we build our maps in a similar decentralized manner, and indeed, was the notion of a map as a central resource really a necessity? Were there advantages to making it an active, representation, rather than a passive data structure?

We have shown that our representation is a viable alternative to the traditional map representations used in mobile robotics. Additionally, we believe it offers certain robustness advantages.

But why even consider such representations? We do not consider an argument of Turing-equivalence sufficient to dissuade us from looking into alternate representations. The same argument could be used to argue that object-oriented programming languages such as C++ are unnecessary since COBOL is Turing equivalent. A much stronger argument needs to be made that distributed representations are not worth studying.

In fact we have a very pragmatic reason for looking at totally distributed representations. (Flynn 1989) introduced the idea of small complete robots built on a single piece of silicon. (Brooks 1987) suggested using the subsumption architecture compiled down to the gate level as a source of intelligence for such robots—the subsumption programs would be written as gates on the same piece of silicon as the actuators, sensors, and power supplies. (Flynn, Brooks & Tavrow 1989*a*) suggest practical ways to implement such *gnat robots*. We expect direct compilation to yield a considerably lower gate count than would a Von Neumann machine programmed to simulate the distributed system. Furthermore, it could rely on much lower speed gates which eases the constraints on the processes used to fabricate the mechanical components of the system.

For this reason we impose an additional constraint on our subsumption programs; at the lowest level of abstraction they must maintain a fixed topology message passing network that can be implemented in silicon in which the total length of interconnect wires between finite state machines is no worse than linear in the total number of machines.

3   The Behavior Language

The subsumption architecture was described initially in (Brooks 1986) and later modified in (Brooks 1989) and (Connell 1989). The subsumption compiler compiles augmented finite state machine (AFSM) descriptions into a special purpose scheduler to simulate parallelism and a set of finite state machine simulation routines. This is a dynamically retargetable compiler that has backends for a number of processors, including the Motorola 68000, the Motorola 68HC11, and the Hitachi 6301. The subsumption compiler takes a source file as input and produces an assembly language program as output.

The behavior language was inspired by (Maes 1989) as a way of grouping AFSMs into more mnaageable units with the capability for whole units being selectively activated or de-activated. In fact, AFSMs are not specified directly, but rather as rule sets of real-time rules which compile into AFSMs in a one-to-one manner. The behavior compiler is machine independent and compiles into an intermediate file of subsumption AFSM specifications. The subsumption compiler can then be used to compile to the various targets. We sometimes call the behavior language the *new subsumption.*

Each augmented finite state machine (AFSM) has a set of registers and a set of timers, or alarm clocks, connected to a conventional finite state machine which can control a combinational network fed by the registers. Registers can be written by attaching input wires to them and sending messages from other machines. The messages get written into the registers by replacing any existing contents. The arrival of a message, or the expiration of a timer, can trigger a change of state in the interior finite state machine. Finite state machine states can either wait on some event, conditionally dispatch to one of two other states based on some combinational predicate on the registers, or compute a combinational function of the registers directing the result either back to one of the registers or to an output of the augmented finite state machine. Some AFSMs connect directly to robot hardware. Sensors deposit their values in certain registers, and certain outputs direct commands to actuators. To arribtrate signals when new peices of network are combined with old, we use the ideas of suppression and inhibition, i.e., subsititution and gating of lower level signals.

Our new behavior language groups multiple processes (each of which usually turns out to be implemented as a single AFSM) into *behaviors*. There can be message passing, suppression, and inhibition between processes within a behavior, and there can be message passing, suppression and inhibition between behaviors. Behaviors act as abstraction barriers, and one behavior cannot reach inside another.

4   The Robot Toto

Toto consists of a three-wheeled circular base, 30cm in diameter, supplied by Real World Interface. The base is capable of following a continuous trajectory with discontinuous velocity. It is position and velocity controllable, and has a built-in motor control processor.

The body of the robot consists of a 12-inch high cylinder mounted on the base supporting a ring of 12 Polaroid ultrasonic ranging sensors (see Figure 16). Given the 30-degree cone of each transducer, the ring covers the entire 360-degree area around the robot. Additionally, the small diameter of the cylinder (15cm) eliminates potential dead-zones in the immediate proximity of the transducers. The only other sensor on the robot is a flux-gate compass supplying four bits of bearing.

Inside the body of the robot is a half-height VME bus, mounted horizontally. It contains a sonar driver board, the main processor board, and the memory and serial port board. The sonar driver uses a Hitachi 6301 microprocessor to multiplex the relays selecting among a dozen transducer lines. The main processor board uses a Hitachi CMOS 68000.

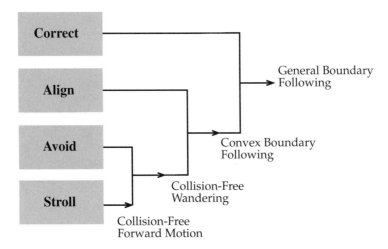

Figure 1: The interaction of the four behaviors resulting in object tracing.

5   Low-Level Navigation

Toto was programmed in the behavior language. Within the layered paradigm of the subsumption architecture, Toto's competences can be divided into three main layers: collision-free wandering, landmark detection, and map learning and path planning.

5.1   Object-Boundary Tracing

Collision-free wandering is Toto's lowest level behavior. It allows the robot to trace out the boundaries of objects in the world by following along their edges. Three threshold distances are used for this purpose: the danger zone, the minimum safe distance, and the edging distance. The robot avoids the danger zone, stays near the minimum safe distance, and keeps within the edging distance of the object whose boundaqry it is tracing. The desired behavior is the emergent result of the interaction of the following four simple navigational rules (Mataric 1989):

Stroll: Sends stop, go, and backup commands to the base, based on Toto's distance from the danger zone. It allows the robot to move safely forward.

Avoid: Changes the robot's heading based on any obstacles within the minimum safe distance thus allowing it to veer around objects. In conjunction with *avoid* it results in an emergent collision-free wandering behavior.

Align: Changes the robot's heading so as to keep it from turning away from the object being followed, and getting out of the edging distance. In conjunction with *stroll* and *avoid* it produces a convex-boundary following behavior.

Correct: Allows the robot to follow concave boundaries by monitoring the side sonars and adjusting the heading appropriately.

Figure 1 shows the interaction of the low-level behaviors resulting in the desired boundary-tracing property of Toto's wandering behavior.

An important characteristic of the wandering algorithm is that it involves no explicit arbitration among the constituent behaviors. Each of the rules is triggered by discrete, mutually-exclusive sensory characteristics, based on the three threshold radii around the robot base. Consequently, arbitration is implicit.

6   Dynamic Landmark Detection

A typical approach to landmark detection with sonar is to match a sonar patter of a location in the world to some stored model of a landmark (Drumheller 1985), (Kuipers 1987). This approach requires the use of odometry and position control which suffer from cumulative errors. Additionally, independent sonar signatures of the same location are unlikely to match exactly due to sensor noise, specularities, and other errors. Rather than attempting to devise a complex static matching algorithm to deal with these problems, we opted for a simple, dynamic approach.

The primary concern in designing a landmark detecting algorithm is the selection of landmarks which can be robustly and repeatedly detected with the given sensors. This led us to choose walls and corridors as frequent landmarks in our environments (office buildings) which are large enough to be reliably detected dynamically, as well as static and unlikely to disappear while the robot is wandering. In contrast to detailed environmental mapping (Chatila & Laumond 1985), (Moravec 1987), the purpose of our robot is to explore and learn the large-scale structure of its environment.

The robustness and reliability of the robot's navigation behaviors allow for a simple, dynamic landmark detecting scheme which circumvents the need for explicit landmark models and matching algorithms. Recall that Toto's low-level navigation algorithm produces a path around the boundaries of objects. The landmark detection algorithm uses this behavior to dynamically extract environmental features from the way the robot is moving.

In our approach, a landmark corresponds to a hypothesis which has gained a high level of confidence. Toto forms hypotheses based on simple rules which rely on the side sonar readings and the compass values. For example, unilateral short sonar readings, coupled with a consistent compass bearing, correspond to an increased confidence in a wall. The algorithm uses a running average to eliminate spurious errors due to sonar specularities or inconsistent compass shifts. It also allows for averaging out dynamic obstacles, such as people walking by, who appear as transient noise.

Spurious inconsistencies in compass direction are averaged out, but large deviations indicate an irregular boundary, and constitute another type of landmark. While they are not necessarily a useful destination point, these landmarks ensure that the robot's list of consecutive locations is continuous in physical space. This, in turn, allows it to optimize paths based on physical rather than only topological distance.

Consistent sensor readings appropriately increase and decrease the landmark confidence levels. When a confidence level reaches a preset threshold, the associated landmark is acknowledged. Confidence levels for individual types of landmarks are maintained in parallel, with independently active monitors. For example, the combination of right and left wall confidences indicates a corridor.

The robustness of the dynamic landmark detection scheme lies in its qualitative nature. It does not rely on position control, which allows the robot to recognize a landmark anywhere along its length. Additionally, it is robust in handling noise and changes in the smaller features in the environment. For instance, adding small and medium-sized furniture or clutter along a wall will not prevent Toto from recognizing it.

7   Spatial Learning and Path Finding

7.1   Active Representations

Once detected, the landmarks need to be stored in some type of a map representation which can later be used for path planning. A graph is a qualitative representation of choice. Instead of a global data structure, we utilize the decentralized nature of the subsumption architecture to implement a distributed graph. In our graph representation, each node is a behavior, consisting of a collection of AFSMs (Mataric 1990b). Equivalent to any other of the robot's behaviors (such as obstacle avoidance and wandering behaviors), each node is an independent agent which corresponds to certain inputs and generates appropriate outputs. In the case of graph nodes, the inputs are landmarks, and the outputs are messages passed to the neighboring nodes, as well as occasional directives to the base.

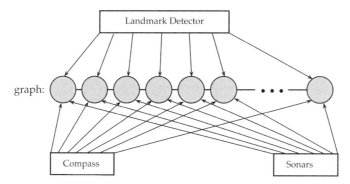

Figure 2: The structure of the distributed graph representation and its connections to other behaviors on the robot.

Since the topology of the graph is statically determined at compile time, the robot is initially given a graph with empty nodes. Exploring the environment corresponds to learning the map by filling the empty nodes. The nodes are interconnected by message wires which allow communication between nearest neighbors in the graph. The chosen graph topology must accommodate any space structure encountered in the physical world since the environment is not known a priori. After considering a variety of possibilities, including two-dimensional near-cartesian grids and routing networks such as the Butterfly and the Tree-mesh, we opted for the simplest yet fully functional solution: a linear list (Figure 2).

7.2   Learning a Map

Whenever a landmark is detected, its type and the corresponding compass bearing are broadcast to the entire graph. Initially, the list of nodes is empty and the first landmark is automatically stored in the first node. (This node is special in that it knows it is the first. This is necessary since there is no global data structure which can perform sequential node allocation.) The node now corresponds to the robot's current position in the graph and is *activated*.

Whenever a node in the graph receives a broadcast landmark, it compares its type, bearing, and a rough position estimate to its own. The matching is a simple comparison which takes into account the duality of each landmark (i.e., a left wall heading south is equivalent to a right wall heading north). Since the matching is performed in parallel, map localization effectively takes constant time, regardless of the size of the graph.

If no graph node reports a match, the landmark is assumed to be new, and should be added to the graph. This is accomplished by storing the new landmark in the graph node adjacent to the currently active position. The active node sends a *wake-up* call to the neighbor who, in turn, is activated, and spreads *deactivation* to its predecessor.

Linear lists bear inherent limitations. Any path that loops back on itself is forced to terminate. This can be remedied if arbitrary connections can be made between any two nodes in the graph. Such a topology is capable of embedding any physically feasible world topology. Since dynamic connections between behaviors are not practical (they require squared connectivity of the graph at compile-time or in hardware fabrication) we use an alternative to a table lookup or a switchboard which simulates arbitrary links. By connecting all behaviors to a switchboard which routes any *jumper* connections appropriately, we gain the full flexibility of dynamic links. We keep the graph connectivity linear in the number of graph nodes by imposing an upper bound on the number of connections from each node. Our experiments have shown empirically that a fanout bound of four (for T-junctions) is fully sufficient for office environments.

The jumpers allow for spreading of expectation analogous to the regular graph connections. Since the graph is expected to be a collection of linear paths adjoining at sparse junctions, the linear list is still the most appropriate data structure. The jumper links allow for appropriate connections between the paths, and their locations correspond to decision points in the environment.

Whenever a node in the graph is active, it spreads *expectation* to its neighbor(s) in the direction of travel. A landmark is considered accurately matched to a node only if that node is expecting. A match without expectation is either false, or an indication that the path contains a loop.

Given the small number of landmark types, it is necessary to employ some alternative method of landmark disambiguation. In general, no totally position-independent method will be able to distinguish between two landmarks of the same qualitative type and compass bearing. This situation is remedied by keeping a very coarse position estimate by integrating the compass bearing over time. This estimate assumes constant velocity of the robot. Although extremely rough, it allows for disambiguation of identical landmarks. (Note that two landmarks of the same type are unlikely to appear in close proximity; e.g. two qualitatively identical left walls must be separated by a detectable space.)

Estimated position is compared to the robot's current rough position estimate whenever a match without expectation occurs. If the positional estimates match within the adjusted error margin, the path is assumed to have looped. At this point a new jumper is added to the graph.

Finally, if the position estimate does not indicate a match, the match is assumed to be false, and the robot proceeds its exploration without updating its position.

7.3   Finding and Executing Paths

The graph containing the landmark information allows the robot to return to any previously visited location. Since there is no global data structure, no classical path planning methods apply. Instead, the same method of activation spreading that is used for communication between graph nodes is used for path planning as well.

The selected *destination* node continuously sends out a *call* to its neighbors. Upon receiving a call, each node propagates it in the appropriate direction. A call from the left it is passed on to the right, and vice versa. Jumper connections use the compass bearing of the previous node to indicate the proper path direction for junctions with higher than binary fanout.

The wave-front of the spreading call eventually reaches the currently active node. At this point, the robot must select the proper direction to pursue toward the goal. Considering the robot's low-level navigation behaviors, it is usually given a choice of proceeding in its current direction, or turning around and going back. The direction of the received call determines which of these options is taken. If the robot is located at a more complex decision point, the jumper connection provides the compass bearing of the desired direction. At each landmark in the graph, the robot makes a decision about its direction of motion. The resulting sequence of actions is the optimal path to the goal.

Without a central data structure, there is no notion of a global path. Each node in the graph contains only local information about the robot's next step. The locality of information eliminates the need for replanning in case the robot strays off the optimal path or becomes lost. Only a change in the goal location generates a new set of local directive for each landmark in the graph.

7.4   Optimizing Paths

Wavefront activation can be viewed as a parallel, or SIMD, version of graph search. Consequently, our algorithm produces the shortest topological path in time linear in the size of the graph. However, the topological path is not necessarily the shortest known physical path. To obtain the actual shortest path, we utilize the notion of *time-as-distance*. Recall that, as the robot traverses the world, it builds up confidences in certain

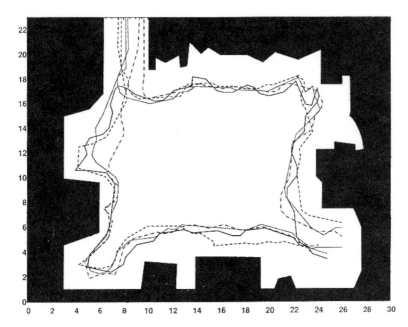

Figure 3: A plot of four independent real runs manifesting consistent object tracing in a cluttered room of an office building. The shown scale is in feet.

landmarks. Confidences are thresholds which correspond to time periods (assuming constant velocity). Thus, each landmark has an implicit length imposed by its threshold. The number of times a single landmark is consecutively matched corresponds to its physical length. We use this rough count as an additional landmark descriptor.

While the call propagates along the wires in the graph, it accrues the size estimates of each landmark it passes. This value contains the length of the traversed path. Each node receives two or more calls. Each active node chooses the call with the smallest length estimate, which results in the physically shortest global path.

8   Experimental Results

8.1   Results of the Navigation Algorithm

Due to the hardware limitations of the ultrasonic transducers, the refresh rate of the full sonar ring is limited to 1Hz. (The firing rate can be doubled with the use of more sophisticated hardware.) The sensor data

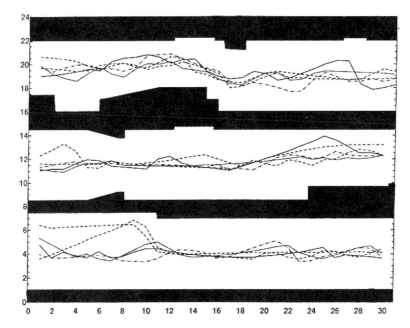

Figure 4: A plot of five real runs showing convergence to the middle of a somewhat cluttered corridor. The shown scale is in feet.

rate imposed a limit on the maximum safe speed for the robot and limited his responsiveness to dynamic obstacles. While incapable of avoiding an obstacle with velocity equal or higher to his, Toto effectively avoids all other static and dynamic obstacles in his environment.

Figure 3 shows five actual runs of the robot in a cluttered room. The data exhibit consistent convergence to a safe path regardless of the robot's starting position. Figure 4 illustrates Toto's performance in a corridor with various clutter along the walls. The robot converges to the center of the corridor because the corridor width is smaller than twice the edging distance. In a wider hallway the robot consistently follows one of the walls.

8.2   Results of the Landmark Detection Algorithm

Figure 5 shows the robot's performance at landmark detection in several independent trials. Repeated test trials generated approximately consistent areas of landmark detection, as indicated in the figure. The data show landmark clustering although the robot's starting position varied in different trials. The environment shown is the same as that used in 3.

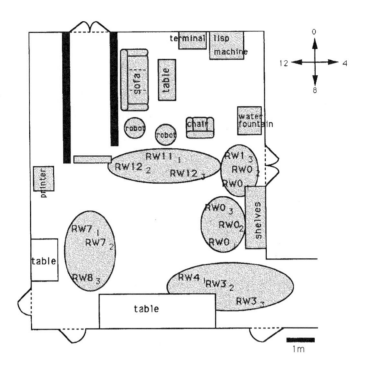

Figure 5: The layout of a sample environment indicating the locations of landmark detection over several independent trials. The data show landmark clustering although the robot's starting position varied in different trials.

Figure 6 illustrates the robot's consistency of landmark detection down a long corridor over five trials. The shaded areas correspond to the same corridor section, illustrating the location of landmark detection going in either direction down the hallway. The shaded and nonshaded ares correspond to the first and second half of the same corridor. While the exact locations of landmark detection vary, the total number of consecutive landmark detection remains relatively constant, resulting in a consistent estimate of the corridor length.

8.3   Results of the Map Learning and Path Finding Algorithms

Figure 7 shows a sample trace of an exploration path through the described environment. Figure 8 shows the resulting graph.

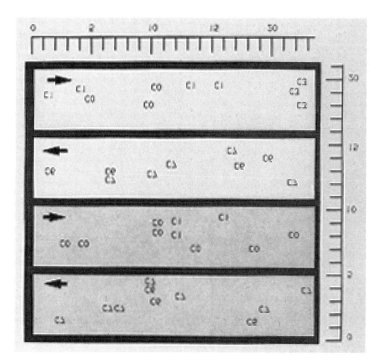

Figure 6: An example of Toto's consistency in corridor detection. The shaded and unshaded areas correspond to two halves of a continuous corridor. The arrows indicate the direction of robot's motion. The exact locations of landmark detection vary, but the total number of detected landmarks remains relatively consistent over independent trials, resulting a good estimate of the corridor length. The scale is in feet, and the locations indicate the exact position of landmark detection, the landmark type, and the associated averaged compass bearing.

The next test demonstrates the robot's ability to return to the initial landmark (i.e., the first node in the list). Figure 9 is a trace showing the processing steps as the robot follows the spreading of activation to reach that destination.

The robot's performance was also tested by imposing static and dynamic obstacles in its path to the goal. Toto's low level navigation behaviors prevent it from colliding with the obstacles while its path planning layer consistently sends it the desired direction. The interaction of these tendencies results in effective veering around obstacles and a persistent pursuit of the direction towards the destination. If an unexpected unsurmountable barrier is imposed between the robot and the

```
node#:   message:
---------------
0        woke-up
         corridor at bearing = 0
0        activated
1        woke-up
         leftwall at bearing = 0
0        deactivated
1        activated
2        woke-up
         leftwall at bearing = 4
1        deactivated
2        activated
3        woke-up
         corridor at bearing = 4
2        deactivated
3        activated
```

Figure 7: A trace illustrating the process of landmark detection and graph construction through node allocation.

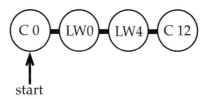

start

Figure 8: The resulting graph.

goal, it could become stuck. The possibility is eliminated by a simple process which prevents the robot from remaining at the same location for too long; the condition causes the termination of the call from the current destination.

In the following experiments we tested the robot's ability to disambiguate among similar landmarks. Figure 10 shows an environment containing potentially ambiguous landmarks. The two corridors are parallel and thus would be perceived as identical. Figure 11 shows the robot's behavior as it detects the second corridor and matches it to the previously encountered landmark. The landmark matches and is expecting, but its positional estimate invalidates the match. Consequently, the new landmark is added to the list. Figure 12 shows the resulting graph.

```
node#:  message:
---------------
0       destination
        send call
1       received call
        passed on call
2       received call
        turned around
2       deactivated
1       activated
        rightwall at bearing = 12
1       received call
0       activated
        corridor at bearing = 8
        destination found!
1       deactivated
```

Figure 9: A trace illustrating the process of returning to the first land-mark by following the direction of the incoming call.

Figure 13 shows a schematic of the previously an environment with strategically added clutter occluding one of the walls. The graph representing the environment is shown in Figure 14 The clutter results in a repeatedly detected uneven boundary which is recorded as a junk-node. The following experiment tested the robot's ability to optimize the path length. We selected a corridor as the goal from a location yielding two paths to it. One of the paths was topologically shorter, while the other contained more nodes but amounted to a shorter physical distance. As illustrated in Figure 15, the robot used the accumulated path distance and chose the physically shorter path to the goal.

9 Conclusion

Our experiments with Toto have demonstrated a number of points. In particular, two questions have been answered affirmatively.

- Map building can be incorporated within the subsumption methodology. Indeed, our experimental results show how its performance can be incrementally improved by adding new pieces of network; first the idea of expectation, then the very coarse position estimate. Map building and path planning worked in simple

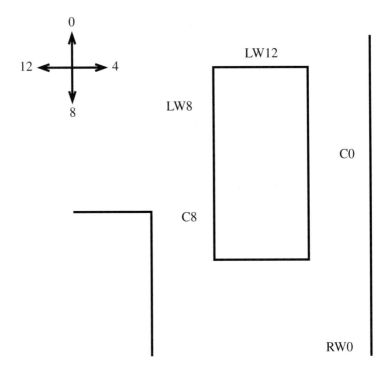

Figure 10: An example of an ambiguous environment.

environments without these improvements. Their addition enabled the robot to function in more complex and ambiguous workspaces.

- Globally consistent maps can be built in a totally distributed manner. In our experiments they were built by a collection of asynchronous independent agents, without the ability to use arbitrary pointers, or other such traditional data structure techniques.

We do not yet know whether there are clear advantages to making maps using an active representation. The ease of integration of the maps with the dynamics of navigation, obstacle avoidance, and path finding is an appealing feature of this representation. Additionally, the representation has a natural ability to integrate temporal aspects of the dynamics since they can use time as its own representation.

In exploring distributed, active representation, we have demonstrated a number of other important points:

- Useful maps do not need to be embedded in the cartesian plane.

```
node#:   message:
---------------
0        woke-up
         rightwall at bearing = 0
0        activated
1        woke-up
         corridor at bearing = 0
0        deactivated
1        activated
2        woke-up
         leftwall at bearing = 12
1        deactivated
2        activated
3        woke-up
         leftwall at bearing = 8
2        deactivated
3        activated
4        woke-up
         corridor at bearing = 8
3        deactivated
4        activated
```

Figure 11: A trace of landmark disambiguation based on expectation.

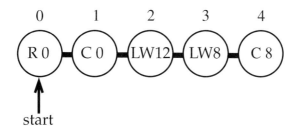

Figure 12: The resulting learned landmark list.

- Coarse position estimates are sufficient to disambiguate landmarks in naturally occurring situations.

- Global orientation estimates need not be at all precise, or accurate, as long as they are locally consistent over time.

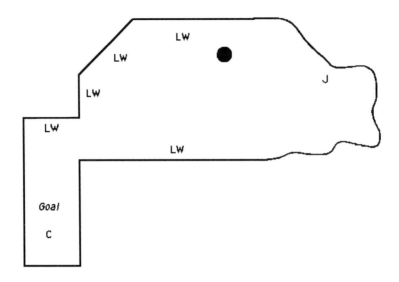

Figure 13: An office environment augmented with strategic clutter used for testing the robot's ability to optimize paths based on physical length. The detected landmarks are indicated, and the schematic approximates the relative scale of the landmarks.

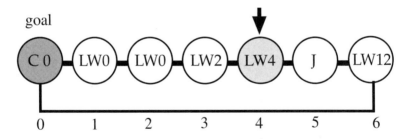

Figure 14: The graph representing the shown environment, with the goal and the current location indicated. Two paths are available from the robot's starting position.

We are greatly encouraged by our work with Toto. We have robustly built and utilized maps with an uncalibrated robot in an unaltered, dynamic, office environment. We used a real, fully autonomous robot, with real sensors and onboard computation. The research taught us that many of the issues adderssed in simulated map building have turned out not to be so important.

```
node#: message:          node#: message:
--------------           --------------
...                      0     destination
0     destination              send call
      send call          1     received call
1     received call            passed on call
      passed on call     ...
6     received call       0     destination
      passed on call            send call
5     received call       6     received call
      passed on call            pass on call
2     received call       1     deactivated
      passed on call      0     activated
3     received call            corridor at bearing = 0
      passed on call            destination found!
4     received call
      waiting
4     received call
      waiting
      turned around
4     deactivated
      rightwall at bearing = 12
```

Figure 15: A trace of execution of the shortest path to the nearest corridor. The paths are available from the robot's starting position, and the physically shorter is executed.

Acknowledgements

Support for this research was provided in part by the Hughes Research Laboratories Artificial Intelligence Center in Malibu, in part by the University Research Initiative under Office of Naval Research contract N00014–86–K–0685, and in part by the Advanced Research Projects Agency under Office of Naval Research contract N00014–85–K–0124.

Figure 16: The robot Toto: A ring of 12 ultrasonic ranging sensors and a compass mounted on a circular base.

CHAPTER 4

. . . .

NEW APPROACHES TO ROBOTICS

By 1991 the behavior-based approach to robotics was starting to be accepted as something more than a passing curiousity. I was invited to summarize the work in the area for Science *which I was glad to do. I have included the resulting paper in the techincal section of this volume as I think it is the clearest description of the important work in the area that I have written, and it positions the rest of the work in this book within a wider context. I almost felt grown up when one of the anonymous reviewers for the paper wrote* "While some of the articles written by Brooks might be considered inflammatory, this one is not."

Abstract. In order to build autonomous robots that can carry out useful work in unstructured environments new approaches have been developed to building intelligent systems. The relationship to traditional academic robotics and traditional artificial intelligence is examined. In the new approaches a tight coupling of sensing to action produces architectures for intelligence that are networks of simple computational elements which are quite broad, but not very deep. Recent work within this approach has demonstrated the use of representations, expectations, plans, goals, and learning, but without resorting to the traditional uses of central, abstractly manipulable or symbolic representations. Perception within these systems is often an active process, and the dynamics of the interactions with the world are extremely important. The question of how to evaluate and compare the new to traditional work still provokes active discussion.

The field of artificial intelligence (AI) tries to make computers do things that, when done by people, are described as having indicated intelligence. The goal of AI has been characterized as both the construction of useful intelligent systems and the understanding of human intelligence (Winston 1984). Since AI's earliest days (Turing 1970) there

Originally appeared in *Science 253*, 1991, pp. 1227–1232.

have been thoughts of building truly intelligent autonomous robots. In academic research circles, work in robotics has influenced work in AI and vice versa.[1]

Over the last seven years a new approach to robotics has been developing in a number of laboratories. Rather than modularize perception, world modeling, planning, and execution, the new approach builds intelligent control systems where many individual modules each directly generate some part of the behavior of the robot. In the purest form of this model each module incorporates its own perceptual, modeling and planning requirements. An arbitration or mediation scheme, built within the framework of the modules, controls which behavior-producing module has control of which part of the robot at any given time.

The work draws its inspirations from neurobiology, ethology, psychophysics, and sociology. The approach grew out of dissatisfactions with traditional robotics and AI, which seemed unable to deliver real-time performance in a dynamic world. The key idea of the new approach is to advance both robotics and AI by considering the problems of building an autonomous agent that physically is an autonomous mobile robot, and which carries out some useful tasks in an environment which has not been specially structured or engineered for it.

There are two subtly different central ideas that are crucial and have led solutions that use behavior-producing modules:

- **Situatedness:** The robots are situated in the world—they do not deal with abstract descriptions, but with the "here" and "now" of the environment which directly influences the behavior of the system.

- **Embodiment:** The robots have bodies and experience the world directly—their actions are part of a dynamic with the world, and the actions have immediate feedback on the robots' own sensations.

An airline reservation system is situated but it is not embodied—it deals with thousands of request per second, and its responses vary as its database changes, but it interacts with the world only through sending and receiving messages. A current generation industrial spray painting robot is embodied but it is not situated—it has a physical extent and its servo routines must correct for its interactions with gravity and noise present in the system, but it does not perceive any aspects of the shape of an object presented to it for painting and simply goes through a pre-programmed series of actions.

---

[1] Applied robotics for industrial automation has not been so closely related to Artificial Intelligence.

This new approach to robotics makes claims on how intelligence should be organized that are radically different from the approach assumed by traditional AI.

1   Traditional Approaches

Although the fields of computer vision, robotics, and AI all have their fairly separate conferences and speciality journals, an implicit intellectual pact between them has developed over the years. None of these fields are experimental sciences in the sense that chemistry, for example, can be an experimental science. Rather, there are two ways in which the fields proceed. One is through the development and synthesis of models of aspects of perception, intelligence, or action, and the other is through the construction of demonstration systems (Cohen 1991). It is relatively rare for an explicit experiment to be done. Rather, the demonstration systems are used to illustrate a particular model in operation. There is no control experiment to compare against, and very little quantitative data extraction or analysis. The intellectual pact between computer vision, robotics, and AI concerns the assumptions that can be made in building demonstration systems. It establishes conventions for what the components of an eventual fully situated and embodied system can assume about each other. These conventions match those used in two critical projects from 1969 to 1972 which set the tone for the next twenty years of research in computer vision, robotics, and AI.

At the Stanford Research Institute (now SRI International) a mobile robot, named *Shakey* was developed (Nilsson 1984). Shakey inhabited a set of specially prepared rooms. It navigated from room to room, trying to satisfy a goal given to it on a teletype. It would, depending on the goal and circumstances, navigate around obstacles consisting of large painted blocks and wedges, push them out of the way, or push them to some desired location. Shakey had an onboard black and white television camera as its primary sensor. An offboard computer analyzed the images, and merged descriptions of what was seen into an existing symbolic logic model of the world in the form of first order predicate calculus. A planning program, STRIPS, operated on those symbolic descriptions of the world to generate a sequence of actions for Shakey. These plans were translated through a series of refinements into calls to atomic actions in fairly tight feedback loops with atomic sensing operations using Shakey's other sensors, such as a bump bar and odometry.

Shakey only worked because of very careful engineering of the environment. Twenty years later, no mobile robot has been demonstrated matching all aspects of Shakey's performance in a more general environment, such as an office environment. The rooms in which Shakey operated were bare except for the large colored blocks and wedges. This made the class of objects that had to be represented very simple. The walls were of a uniform color, and carefully lighted, with dark rubber baseboards, making clear boundaries with the lighter colored floor. This meant that very simple and robust vision of trihedral corners between two walls and the floor could be used for relocalizing the robot in order to correct for drift in the odometric measurements. The blocks and wedges were painted different colors on different planar surfaces. This ensured that it was relatively easy, especially in the good lighting provided, to find edges in the images separating the surfaces, and thus to identify the shape of the polyhedron. Blocks and wedges were relatively rare in the environment, eliminating problems due to partial obscurations.

At MIT, a camera system and a robot manipulator arm were programmed to perceive an arrangement of white wooden blocks against a black background, and to build a copy of the structure from additional blocks. This was called the *copy-demo* (Winston 1972). The programs to do this were very specific to the world of blocks with rectangular sides, and would not have worked in the presence of simple curved objects, rough texture on the blocks, or without carefully controlled lighting. Nevertheless it reinforced the idea that a complete three dimensional description of the world could be extracted from a visual image. It legitimized the work of others, such as Winograd (1972), whose programs worked in a make-believe world of blocks—if one program could be built which understood such a world completely and could also manipulate that world, then it seemed that programs which assumed that abstraction could in fact be connected to the real world without great difficulty.

The role of computer vision was "given a two-dimensional image, infer the objects that produced it, including their shapes, positions, colors, and sizes" (Charniak & McDermott 1984). This attitude lead to an emphasis on recovery of three dimensional shape (Marr 1982), from monocular and stereo images. A number of demonstration recognition and location systems were built, such as those of Brooks (1984b) and Grimson (1990), although they tended not to rely on using three dimensional shape recovery.

The role of AI was to take descriptions of the world (though usually not as geometric as vision seemed destined to deliver, or as robotics seemed to need) and manipulate them based on a data-base of knowledge about how the world works in order to solve problems, make plans, and produce explanations. These high-level aspirations have very rarely been embodied by connection to either computer vision systems or robotics devices.

The role of robotics was to deal with the physical interactions with the world. As robotics adopted the idea of having a complete three dimensional world model, a number of subproblems became standardized. One was to plan a collision-free path through the world model for a manipulator arm, or for a mobile robot—see the article by Yap (1985) for a survey of the literature. Another was to understand forward kinematics and dynamics—given a set of joint or wheel torques as functions over time, what path would the robot hand or body follow. A more useful, but harder, problem is inverse kinematics and dynamics—given a desired trajectory as a function of time, for instance one generated by a collision-free path planning algorithm, compute the set of joint or wheel torques that should be applied to follow that path within some prescribed accuracy (Brady, Hollerbach, Johnson & Lozano-Pérez 1982).

It became clear after a while that perfect models of the world could not be obtained from sensors, or even CAD data-bases. Some attempted to model the uncertainty explicitly (Brooks 1982), (Chatila & Laumond 1985), and found strategies that worked in its presence, while others moved away from position-based techniques to force-based planning, at least in the manipulator world (Lozano-Pérez, Mason & Taylor 1984). Ambitious plans were laid for combining many of the pieces of research over the years into a unified planning and execution system for robot manipulators (Lozano-Pérez & Brooks 1984), but after years of theoretical progress and long-term impressive engineering, the most advanced systems are still far from the ideal (Lozano-Pérez, Jones, Mazer & O'Donnell 1989).

These approaches, along with those in the mobile robot domain (Moravec 1983), (Simmons & Krotkov 1991), shared the *sense-model-plan-act* framework, where an iteration through the cycle could often take 15 minutes or more (Moravec 1983), (Lozano-Pérez et al. 1989).

2 The New Approach

Driven by a dissatisfaction with the performance of robots in dealing with the real world, and concerned that the complexity of runtime modeling of the world was getting out of hand, a number of people somewhat independently began around 1984 rethinking the general problem of organizing intelligence. It seemed a reasonable requirement that intelligence be reactive to dynamic aspects of the environment, that a mobile robot operate on time scales similar to those of animals and humans, and that intelligence be able to generate robust behavior in the face of uncertain sensors, an unpredictable environment, and a changing world.

Some of the key realizations about the organization of intelligence were as follows:

- Agre and Chapman at MIT claimed that most of what people do in their day to day lives is not problem-solving or planning, but rather it is routine activity in a relatively benign, but certainly dynamic, world. Furthermore the representations an agent uses of objects in the world need not rely on naming those objects with symbols that the agent possesses, but rather can be defined through interactions of the agent with the world (Agre & Chapman 1987), (Agre & Chapman 1990).

- Rosenschein and Kaelbling at SRI International (and later at Teleos Research) pointed out that an observer can legitimately talk about an agent's beliefs and goals, even though the agent need not manipulate symbolic data structures at run time. A formal symbolic specification of the agent's design can be compiled away, yielding efficient robot programs (Rosenschein & Kaelbling 1986a), (Kaelbling & Rosenschein 1990).

- Brooks at MIT argued that in order to really test ideas of intelligence it is important to build complete agents which operate in dynamic environments using real sensors. Internal world models which are complete representations of the external environment, besides being impossible to obtain, are not at all necessary for agents to act in a competent manner. Many of the actions of an agent are quite separable—coherent intelligence can emerge from independent subcomponents interacting in the world (Brooks 1986), (Brooks 1990c), (Brooks 1991c).

All three groups produced implementations of these ideas, using as their medium of expression a network of simple computational elements, hardwired together, connecting sensors to actuators, with a small amount of state maintained over clock ticks.

Agre and Chapman demonstrated their ideas by building programs for playing video games. The first such program was called Pengi, and played a concurrently running video game program, with one protagonist and many opponents which can launch dangerous projectiles. Figure 1 shows the schematic architecture for Pengi. There are two components to the architecture—a visual routine processor (VRP) which provides input to the system, and a network of standard logic gates which can be categorized into three components: *aspect detectors, action suggestors* and *arbiters*. The system plays the game from the same point of view as a human playing a video game, not from the point of view of the

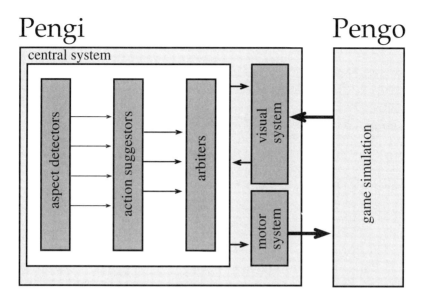

Figure 1: The Pengi system (Agre & Chapman 1987) played a video game called Pengo. The control system consisted of a network of logic gates, organized into a visual system, a central system, and a motor system. The only state was within the visual system. The network within the central system was organized into three components: an aspect detector subnetwork, an action suggestor subnetwork and an arbiter subnetwork.

protagonist within the game. However, rather than analyze a visual bit map, the Pengi program is presented with an iconic version. The VRP implements a version of Ullman's visual routines theory (Ullman 1984), where markers from a set of six are placed on certain icons, and follow them. Operators can place a marker on the *nearest-opponent*, for example, and it will track that opponent even when it is no longer the nearest. The placement of these markers were the only state in the system. Projection operators let the player predict the consequences of actions, for instance, launching a projectile. The results of the VRP are analyzed by the first part of the central network, and describe certain aspects of the world. In the mind of the designer, output signals designate such things as "the protagonist is moving", "a projectile from the north is about to hit the protaganist", and so on. The next part of the network takes boolean combinations of such signals to suggest actions, and the third stage uses a fixed priority scheme (that is, it never learns) to select the next action. The use of these types of *deictic* representations was a key move away from the traditional AI approach of dealing only with named individuals in the world (for instance, *opponent-27* rather than the deictic *the-opponent-which-is-closest-to-the-protagonist*, whose objective identity may change over time) and lead to very different requirements on the sort of reasoning that was necessary to perform well in the world.

Rosenschein and Kaelbling used a robot named Flakey, which operated in the regular and unaltered office areas of SRI in the vicinity of the special environment for Shakey that had been built two decades earlier. Their architecture was split into a perception subnetwork, and an action subnetwork. The networks were ultimately constructed of standard logic gates and delay elements (with feedback loops these provided the network with state), although the programmer wrote at a much higher level of abstraction—in terms of goals that the robot should try to satisfy. By formally specifying the relationships between sensors and effectors and the world, and by using off-line symbolic computation, Rosenschein and Kaelbling's high-level languages were used to generate provably correct, real-time programs for Flakey. The technique may be limited by the computational complexity of the symbolic compilation process as the programs get larger and by the validity of their models of sensors and actuators.

Brooks developed the *subsumption architecture*, which deliberately changed the modularity from the traditional AI approach. Figure 2 shows a vertical decomposition into task achieving behaviors rather than information processing modules. This architecture was used on robots which explore, build maps, have an onboard manipulator, walk, interact with people, navigate visually, and learn to coordinate many conflicting internal behaviors. The implementation substrate consists of networks of message-passing augmented finite state machines (AFSMs). The messages are sent over predefined 'wires' from a specific transmitting to a specific receiving AFSM. The messages are simple numbers (typically 8 bits) whose meaning depends on the designs of both the transmitter and the receiver. An AFSM has additional registers which hold the most recent incoming message on any particular wire. The registers can have their values fed into a local combinatorial circuit to produce new values for registers or to provide an output message. The network of AFSMs is totally asynchronous, but individual AFSMs can have fixed duration monostables which provide for dealing with the flow of time in the outside world. The behavioral competence of the system is improved by adding more behavior-specific network to the existing network. This process is called *layering*. This is a simplistic and crude analogy to evolutionary development. As with evolution, at every stage of the development the systems are tested. Each of the layers is a behavior-producing

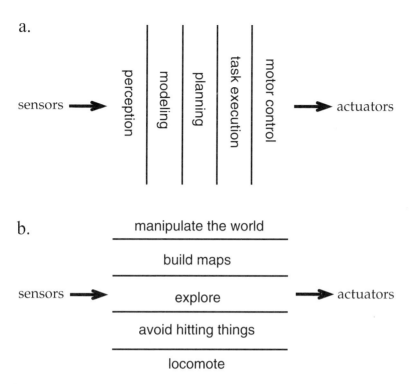

a.

sensors ➤ perception | modeling | planning | task execution | motor control ➤ actuators

b.

manipulate the world

build maps

sensors ➤ explore ➤ actuators

avoid hitting things

locomote

Figure 2: The traditional decomposition for an intelligent control system within AI is to break processing into a chain of information processing modules (a) proceeding from sensing to action. In the new approach (b), the decomposition is in terms of behavior generating modules each of which connects sensing to action. Layers are added incrementally, and newer layers may depend on earlier layers operating successfully, but do not call them as explicit subroutines.

piece of network in its own right, although it may implicitly rely on presence of earlier pieces of network. For instance, an *explore* layer does not need to explicitly avoid obstacles, as the designer knows that the existing *avoid* layer will take care of it. A fixed priority arbitration scheme is used to handle conflicts.

These architectures were radically different from those in use in the robotics community at the time. There was no central model of the world explicitly represented within the systems. There was no implicit separation of data and computation—they were both distributed over the same network of elements. There were no pointers, and no easy

way to implement them, as there is in symbolic programs. Any search
space had to be a bounded in size *a priori*, as search nodes could not be
dynamically created and destroyed during a search process. There was
no central locus of control. In general, the separation into perceptual
system, central system, and actuation system was much less distinct
than in previous approaches, and indeed in these systems there was an
intimate intertwining of aspects of all three of these capabilities. There
was no notion of one process calling on another as a subroutine. Rather,
the networks were designed so that results of computations would simply
be available at the appropriate location when needed. The boundary
between computation and the world was harder to draw as the systems
relied heavily on the dynamics of their interactions with the world to
produce their results. For instance, sometimes a physical action by the
robot would trigger a change in the world which would be perceived and
cause the next action, in contrast to directly executing the two actions
in sequence.

Most of the behavior-based robotics work has been done with implemented physical robots. Some has been done purely in software (Agre &
Chapman 1987), not as a simulation of a physical robot, but rather as a
computational experiment in an entirely make-believe domain to explore
certain critical aspects of the problem. This contrasts with traditional
robotics where many demonstrations are performed only on software
simulations of robots.

3   Areas of Work

Perhaps inspired by this early work and also by (Minsky 1986)'s rather
more theoretical Society of Mind ideas on how the human mind is organized, various groups around the world have pursued behavior-based
approaches to robotics over the last few years. The following is a survey
some of that work and relates it to the key issues and problems for the
field.

One of the shortcomings in earlier approaches to robotics and AI
was that reasoning was so slow that systems that were built could not
respond to a dynamic real world. A key feature of the new approaches
to robotics is that the programs are built with short connections between sensors and actuators, making it plausible, in principle at least,
to respond quickly to changes in the world.

The first demonstration of the subsumption architecture was on the
robot *Allen* (Brooks 1986). The robot was almost entirely reactive,
using sonar readings to keep away from moving people and other moving
obstacles, while not colliding with static obstacles. It also had a non-

reactive higher level layer that would select a goal to head towards, and then proceed in that direction while the lower level reactive layer took care of avoiding obstacles. It thus combined non-reactive capabilities with reactive ones. More importantly, it used exactly the same sorts of computational mechanism to do both. In looking at the network of the combined layers there was no obvious partition into lower and higher level components based on the type of information flowing on the connections, or the finite state machines that were the computational elements. To be sure, there was a difference in function between the two layers, but there was no need to introduce any centralization or explicit representations to achieve a later, higher-level process having useful and effective influence over an earlier, lower level.

The subsumption architecture was generalized (Horswill & Brooks 1988) so that some of the connections between processing elements could implement a *retina bus*, a cable that transmitted partially processed images from one site to another within the system. It applied simple difference operators, and region growing techniques, to segment the visual field into moving and non-moving parts, and into floor and non-floor parts. Location, but not identity of the segmented regions, was used to implement image-coordinate-based navigation. All the visual techniques were known to be very unreliable on single grey-level images, but by having redundant techniques operating in parallel and rapidly switching between them, robustness was achieved. The robot was able to follow corridors and moving objects in real time, with very little computational resources by modern computer vision standards.

This idea of using redundancy over many images is in contrast to the approach in traditional computer vision research of trying to extract the maximal amount of information from a single image, or pair of images. This lead to trying to get complete depth maps over a full field of view from a single pair of stereo images. Ballard (1989) points out that humans do not do this, but rather servo their two eyes to verge on a particular point and then extract relative depth information about that point. With this and many other examples he points out that an active vision system, that is, one with control over its cameras, can work naturally in object centered-coordinates, whereas a passive vision system, that is, one which has no control over its cameras, is doomed to work in viewer-centered coordinates. A large effort is underway at Rochester to exploit behavior-based or animate vision. Dickmanns & Graefe (1988) in Munich have used redundancy from multiple images, and multiple feature windows which track relevant features between images, while virtually ignoring the rest of the image, to control a truck driving on a freeway at over 100 km/h.

Figure 3: Genghis is a six-legged robot measuring 35cm in length. Each rigid leg is attached at a shoulder joint with two degrees of rotational freedom, each driven by a model airplane position controllable servo motor. The sensors are pitch and roll inclinometers, two collision sensitive antennae, six forward looking passive pyroelectric infrared sensors, and crude force measurements from the servo loops of each motor. There are four onboard 8 bit micro-processors, three of which handle motor and sensor signals, and one of which runs the subsumption architecture.

Although predating the emphasis on behavior-based robots, (Raibert 1986)'s hopping robots fit their spirit. Traditional walking robots are given a desired trajectory for their body and then appropriate leg motions are computed. In Raibert's one-, two-, and four-legged machines, he decomposed the problem into independently controlling the hopping height of a leg, its forward velocity, and the body attitude. The motion of the robot's body emerges from the interactions of these loops and the world. Using subsumption, Brooks programmed a six legged robot, *Genghis* (Figure 3) to walk over rough terrain (Brooks 1989). In this case, layers of behaviors implemented first the ability to stand up, then to walk without feedback, then to adjust for rough terrain and obstacles by means of force feedback, then to modulate for this accommodation based on pitch and roll inclinometers. The trajectory for the body is not specified explicitly, nor is there any hierarchical control. The robot successfully navigates rough terrain with very little computation. Figure 4

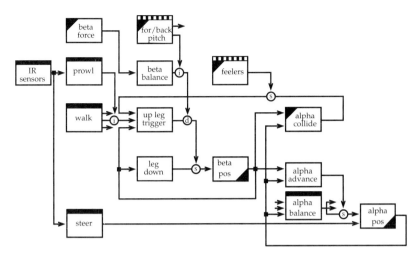

Figure 4: The subsumption network to control Genghis consists of 57 augmented finite state machines, with 'wires' connecting them that pass small integers as messages. The elements without bands on top are repeated six times, once for each leg. The network was built incrementally starting in the lower right corner, and new layers were added, roughly towards the upper left corner, increasing the behavioral repetoire at each stage.

shows the wiring diagram of the 57 augmented finite state machines which controlled it.

There have been a number of behavior-based experiments with robot manipulators. Connell (1989) used a collection of 17 AFSMs to control a two degree of freedom arm mounted on a mobile base. When parked in front of a soda can, whether at floor level or on a table top, the arm was able to reliably find it and pick it up, despite other clutter in front of and under the can, using its local sensors to direct its search. All the AFSMs had sensor values as their only inputs and outputted actuator commands which then went through a fixed priority arbitration network to control the arm and hand. In this case, there was no communication between the AFSMs, and the system was completely reactive to its environment. Malcolm & Smithers (1990) at Edinburgh report a hybrid assembly system. A traditional AI planner produces plans for a robot manipulator to assemble the components of some artifact, and a behavior-based system executes the plan steps. The key idea is to give the higher level planner robust primitives which can do more than carry out simple motions, thus making the planning problem easier.

Representation is a cornerstone topic in traditional AI. At MIT, Mataric (1990a) has recently introduced active representations into the subsumption architecture. Identical subnetworks of AFSMs are the representational units.   In experiments with a sonar-based office-environment navigating robot named *Toto*, landmarks were broadcast to the representational substrate as they were encountered. A previously unallocated subnetwork would become the representation for that landmark, and then take care of noting topological neighborhood relationships, setting up expectation as the robot moved through previously encountered space, spreading activation energy for path planning to multiple goals, and directing the robot's motion during goal seeking behavior when in the vicinity of the landmark. In this approach the representations and the ways in which they are used are inseparable—it all happens in the same computational units within the network. Nehmzow & Smithers (1991) at Edinburgh have also experimented with including representations of landmarks, but their robots operated in a simpler world of plywood enclosures. They used self-organizing networks to represent knowledge of the world, and appropriate influence on the current action of the robot. Additionally, the Edinburgh group has done a number of experiments with reactivity of robots, and with group dynamics amongst robots using a Lego-based rapid prototyping system that they have developed.

Many of the early behavior-based approaches used a fixed priority scheme to decide which behavior could control a particular actuator at which time.   At Hughes, an alternative voting scheme was produced (Payton 1986) to enable a robot to take advantage of the outputs of many behaviors simultaneously.   At Brussels a scheme for selectively activating and de-activating complete behaviors was developed by Maes (1989), based on spreading activation within the network itself. This scheme was further developed at MIT and used to program *Toto* amongst other robots. In particular, it was used to provide a learning mechanism on the six legged robot *Genghis*, so that it could learn to coordinate its leg lifting behaviors, based on negative feedback from falling down (Maes & Brooks 1990).

Very recently there has been work at IBM (Mahadevan & Connell 1990) and Teleos Research (Kaelbling 1990) using Q-learning (Watkins 1989) to modify the behavior of robots. There seem to be drawbacks with the convergence time for these algorithms, but more experimentation on real systems is needed.

A number of researchers from traditional robotics (Arkin 1990) and AI (Mitchell 1990), (Malkin & Addanki 1990), have adopted the philosophies of the behavior-based approaches as the bottom of two level system as shown in Figure 5. The idea is to let a reactive behavior-based sys-

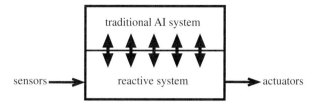

Figure 5: A number of projects involve combining a reactive system, linking sensors and actuators, with a traditional AI system that does symbolic reasoning in order to tune the parameters of the situated component.

tem take care of the real time issues involved with interacting with the world while a more traditional AI system sits on top, making longer term executive decisions that effect the policies executed by the lower level. Others (Brooks 1991*b*) argue that purely behavior-based systems are all that are needed.

4 Evaluation

It has been difficult to come to grips with how to evaluate work done under the banner of the new approaches to robotics. Its proponents have often argued on the basis of performance of systems built within its style. But performance is hard to evaluate, and there has been much criticism that the approach is both unprincipled and will not scale well. The unprincipled argument comes from comparisons to traditional academic robotics, and the scaling argument comes from traditional AI. Both these disciplines have established but informal criteria for what makes a good and respectable piece of research.

Traditional academic robotics has worked in a somewhat perfect domain. There are CAD-like models of objects and robots, and a modeled physics of how things interact (Lozano-Pérez et al. 1984). Much of the work is in developing algorithms which guarantee certain classes of results in the modeled world. Verifications are occasionally done with real robots (Lozano-Pérez et al. 1989), but typically those trials are nowhere nearly as complicated as the examples which can be handled in simulation. The sticking point seems to be in how well the experimenters are able to coax the physical robots to match the physics of the simulated robots.

For the new approaches to robotics however, where the emphasis is on understanding and exploiting the dynamics of interactions with the world, it makes sense to measure and analyze the systems as they are situated in the world. In the same way modern ethology has prospered by studying animals in their native habitats, not just in Skinner boxes. For instance, a particular sensor, under ideal experimental conditions, may have a particular resolution. Suppose the sensor is a sonar. Then to measure its resolution an experiment will be set up where a return signal from the test article is sensed, and the resolution will be compared against measurements of distance using a ruler or some such device. The experiment might be done for a number of different surface types. But when that sensor is installed on a mobile robot, situated in a cluttered, dynamically changing world, the return signals that reach the sensor may come from many possible sources. The object nearest the sensor may not be made of one of the tested materials. It may be at such an angle that the sonar pulse acts as though it were a mirror, and so the sonar sees a secondary reflection. The secondary lobes of the sonar might detect something in a cluttered situation where there was no such interference in the clean experimental situation. One of the main points of the new approaches to robotics is that these effects are extremely important on the overall behavior of a robot. They are also extremely difficult to model. So the traditional robotics approach of proving correctness in an abstract model may be somewhat meaningless in the new approaches. We need to find ways of formalizing our understanding the dynamics of interactions with the world so that we can build theoretical tools which will let us make predictions about the performance of our new robots.

In traditional AI there are many classes of research contributions (as distinct from application deployment). Two of the most popular are described here. One is to provide a formalism that is consistent for some level of description of some aspect of the world, for example, qualitative physics, stereotyped interactions between speakers, or categorizations or taxonomies of animals. This class of work does not necessarily require any particular results, theorems, or working programs, to be judged adequate; the formalism is the important contribution. A second class of research takes some input representation of some aspects of a situation in the world, and makes a of prediction. For example, it might be in the form of a plan to effect some change in the world, in the form of the drawing of an analogy with some schema in a library in order to deduce some non-obvious fact, or it might be in the form of providing some expert-level advice. These research contributions do not have to be tested in situated systems—there is an implicit understanding amongst researchers about what is reasonable to 'tell' the systems in the input data.

In the new approaches there is a much stronger feeling that the robots must find everything out about their particular world by themselves. This is not to say that *a priori* knowledge can not be incorporated into a robot, but that it must be non-specific to the particular location that the robot will be tested in. Given the current capabilities of computer perception, this forces behavior-based robots to operate in a much more uncertain, and much more coarsely described world than traditional AI systems operating in simulated, imagined worlds. The new systems can therefore seem to have much more limited abilities. I would argue (Brooks 1991*b*), however, that the traditional systems operate in a way which will never be transportable to the real worlds that the situated behavior-based robots already inhabit.

The new approaches to robotics have garnered a lot of interest, and many people are starting to work on their various aspects. Some are trying to build systems using only the new approaches, others are trying to integrate them with existing work, and of course there is much work continuing in the traditional style. The community is divided on the appropriate approach, and more work needs to be done in making comparisons in order to understand the issues better.

Acknowledgements

Supported in part by the University Research Initiative under Office of Naval Research contract N00014–86–K–0685, in part by the Defense Advanced Research Projects Agency under Office of Naval Research contract N00014–85–K–0124, in part by the Hughes Artificial Intelligence Center, in part by Siemens Corporation, and in part by Mazda Corporation.

PART II

PHILOSOPHY

CHAPTER 5

· ·

INTELLIGENCE WITHOUT REPRESENTATION

After the physical success with the robot reported in the paper in chapter 1, I tried to look at the bigger picture of why things were working so well. The result was this paper. An early draft of this was circulated in 1986, and the paper was in its current form by April 1987. However it was not published for many years. It was turned down by many conferences and many journals. The reviews were withering: "There is no scientific content here; little in the way of reasoned argument, as opposed to petulant assertions and non-sequiturs, and ample evidence of ignorance of the literature on these questions." *But the underground versions were widely referenced, and made it on required reading lists for Artificial Intelligence graduate programs. Eventually the world changed and the paper was printed unaltered in the most esteemed journal for Artificial Intelligence. I must admit that the title is a little inflammatory—a careful reading shows that I mean intelligence without* conventional *representation, rather than without any representation at all. This has lead to much confusion about my position and I regret that, but I still like the title.*

Abstract. Artificial intelligence research has foundered on the issue of representation. When intelligence is approached in an incremental manner, with strict reliance on interfacing to the real world through perception and action, reliance on representation disappears. In this paper we outline our approach to incrementally building complete intelligent Creatures. The fundamental decomposition of the intelligent system is not into independent information processing units which must interface with each other via representations. Instead, the intelligent system is decomposed into independent and parallel activity producers which all interface directly to the world through perception and action, rather than interface to each other particularly much. The notions of

Originally appeared in the *Artificial Intelligence Journal 47*, 1991, pp. 139–160.

central and peripheral systems evaporate–everything is both central and peripheral. Based on these principles we have built a very successful series of mobile robots which operate without supervision as Creatures in standard office environments.

1   Introduction

Artificial intelligence started as a field whose goal was to replicate human level intelligence in a machine.

Early hopes diminished as the magnitude and difficulty of that goal was appreciated. Slow progress was made over the next 25 years in demonstrating isolated aspects of intelligence. Recent work has tended to concentrate on commercializable aspects of "intelligent assistants" for human workers.

No one talks about replicating the full gamut of human intelligence any more. Instead we see a retreat into specialized subproblems, such as ways to represent knowledge, natural language understanding, vision or even more specialized areas such as truth maintenance systems or plan verification. All the work in these subareas is benchmarked against the sorts of tasks humans do within those areas. Amongst the dreamers still in the field of AI (those not dreaming about dollars, that is), there is a feeling. that one day all these pieces will all fall into place and we will see "truly" intelligent systems emerge.

However, I, and others, believe that human level intelligence is too complex and little understood to be correctly decomposed into the right subpieces at the moment and that even if we knew the subpieces we still wouldn't know the right interfaces between them. Furthermore, we will never understand how to decompose human level intelligence until we've had a lot of practice with simpler level intelligences.

In this paper I therefore argue for a different approach to creating artificial intelligence:

- We must incrementally build up the capabilities of intelligent systems, having complete systems at each step of the way and thus automatically ensure that the pieces and their interfaces are valid.

- At each step we should build complete intelligent systems that we let loose in the real world with real sensing and real action. Anything less provides a candidate with which we can delude ourselves.

We have been following this approach and have built a series of autonomous mobile robots. We have reached an unexpected conclusion (C) and have a rather radical hypothesis (H).

(C) When we examine very simple level intelligence we find that explicit representations and models of the world simply get in the way. It turns out to be better to use the world as its own model.

(H) Representation is the wrong unit of abstraction in building the bulkiest parts of intelligent systems.

Representation has been the central issue in artificial intelligence work over the last 15 years only because it has provided an interface between otherwise isolated modules and conference papers.

2   The Evolution of Intelligence

We already have an existence proof of, the possibility of intelligent entities: human beings. Additionally, many animals are intelligent to some degree. (This is a subject of intense debate, much of which really centers around a definition of intelligence.) They have evolved over the 4.6 billion year history of the earth.

It is instructive to reflect on the way in which earth-based biological evolution spent its time. Single-cell entities arose out of the primordial soup roughly 3.5 billion years ago. A billion years passed before photosynthetic plants appeared. After almost another billion and a half years, around 550 million years ago, the first fish and Vertebrates arrived, and then insects 450 million years ago. Then things started moving fast. Reptiles arrived 370 million years ago, followed by dinosaurs at 330 and mammals at 250 million years ago. The first primates appeared 120 million years ago and the immediate predecessors to the great apes a mere 18 million years ago. Man arrived in roughly his present form 2.5 million years ago. He invented agriculture a mere 10,000 years ago, writing less than 5000 years ago and "expert" knowledge only over the last few hundred years,

This suggests that problem solving behavior, language, expert knowledge and application, and reason, are all pretty simple once the essence of being and reacting are available. That essence is the ability to move around in a dynamic environment, sensing the surroundings to a degree sufficient to achieve the necessary maintenance of life and reproduction. This part of intelligence is where evolution has concentrated its time–it is much harder.

I believe that mobility, acute vision and the ability to carry out survivalrelated tasks in a dynamic environment provide a necessary basis for the development of true intelligence. Moravec (Moravec 1984a) argues this same case rather eloquently.

Human level intelligence has provided us with an existence proof but we must be careful about what the lessons are to be gained from it.

2.1   A Story

Suppose it is the 1890s. Artificial flight is the glamor subject in science, engineering, and venture capital circles. A bunch of AF researchers are miraculously transported by a time machine to the 1980s for a few hours. They spend the whole time in the passenger cabin of a commercial passenger Boeing 747 on a medium duration flight.

Returned to the 1890s they feel vigorated, knowing that AF is possible on a grand scale. They immediately set to work duplicating what they have seen. They make great progress in designing pitched seats, double pane windows, and know that if only they can figure out those weird "plastics" they will have their grail within their grasp. (A few connectionists amongst them caught a glimpse of an engine with its cover off and they are preoccupied with inspirations from that experience.)

3   Abstraction as a Dangerous Weapon

Artificial intelligence researchers are fond of pointing out that AI is often denied its rightful successes. The popular story goes that when nobody has any good idea of how to solve a particular sort of problem (e.g., playing chess) it is known as an AI problem. When an algorithm developed by AI researchers successfully tackles such a problem, however, AI detractors claim that since the problem was solvable by an algorithm, it wasn't really an AI problem after all. Thus AI never has any successes. But have you ever heard of an AI failure?

I claim that AI researchers are guilty of the same (self) deception. They partition the problems they work on into two components. The AI component, which they solve, and the non-AI component which, they don't solve. Typically, AI "succeeds" by defining the parts of the problem that are unsolved as not AI. The principal mechanism for this partitioning is abstraction. Its application is usually considered part of good science, not, as it is in fact used in AI, as a mechanism for self-delusion. In AI, abstraction is usually used to factor out all aspects of perception and motor skills. I argue below that these are the hard problems solved by intelligent systems, and further that the shape of solutions to these problems constrains greatly the correct solutions of the small pieces of intelligence which remain.

Early work in AI concentrated on games, geometrical problems, symbolic algebra, theorem proving, and other formal systems (e.g., (Feigenbaum & Feldman 1963), (Minsky 1968)). In each case the semantics of the domains were fairly simple.

In the late sixties and early seventies the blocks world became a popular domain for AI research. It had a uniform and simple semantics.

The key to success was to represent the state of the world completely and explicitly. Search techniques could then be used for planning within this well-understood world. Learning could also be done within the blocks world; there were only a few simple concepts worth learning and they could be captured by enumerating the set of subexpressions which must be contained in any formal description of a world including an instance of the concept. The blocks world was even used for vision research and mobile robotics, as it provided strong constraints on the perceptual processing necessary (Nilsson 1984).

Eventually criticism surfaced that the blocks world was a "toy world" and that within it there were simple special purpose solutions to what should be considered more general problems. At the same time there was a funding crisis within AI (both in the US and the UK, the two most active places for AI research at the time). AI researchers found themselves forced to become relevant. They moved into more complex domains, such as trip planning, going to a restaurant, medical diagnosis, etc.

Soon there was a new slogan: "Good representation is the key to AI" (e.g., *conceptually efficient programs* in (Bobrow & Brown 1975)). The idea was that by representing only the pertinent facts explicitly, the semantics of a world (which on the surface was quite complex) were reduced to a simple closed system once again. Abstraction to only the relevant details thus simplified the problems. Consider a chair for example. While the following two characterizations are true:

(CAN (SIT-ON PERSON CHAIR))

(CAN (STAND-ON PERSON CHAIR))

there is much more to the concept of a chair. Chairs have some flat (maybe) sitting place, with perhaps a back support. They have a range of possible sizes, requirements on strength, and a range of possibilities in shape. They often have some sort of covering material, unless they are made of wood, metal or plastic. They sometimes are soft in particular places. They can come from a range of possible styles. In particular the concept of what is a chair is hard to characterize simply. There is certainly no AI vision program which can find arbitrary chairs in arbitrary images; they can at best find one particular type of chair in carefully selected images.

This characterization, however, is perhaps the correct AI representation of solving certain problems; e.g., a person sitting on a chair in a room is hungry and can see a banana hanging from the ceiling just out of reach. Such problems are never posed to AI systems by showing them a photo of the scene. A person (even a young child) can make the right interpretation of the photo and suggest a plan of action. For AI planning systems however, the experimenter is required to abstract away most of the details to form a simple description in terms of atomic concepts such as PERSON, CHAIR and BANANAS.

But this abstraction is the essence of intelligence and the hard part of the problems being solved. Under the current scheme the abstraction is done by the researchers leaving little for the AI programs to do but search. A truly intelligent program would study the photograph, perform the abstraction and solve the problem.

The only input to most AI programs is a restricted set of simple assertions deduced from the real data by humans. The problems of recognition, spatial understanding, dealing with sensor noise, partial models, etc. are all ignored. These problems are relegated to the realm of input black boxes. Psychophysical evidence suggests they are all intimately tied up with the representation of the world used by an intelligent system.

There is no clean division between perception (abstraction) and reasoning in the real. world. The brittleness of current AI systems attests to this fact. For example, MYCIN (Shortliffe 1976) is an expert at diagnosing human bacterial infections, but it really has no model of what a human (or any living creature) is or how they work, or what are plausible things to happen to a human. If told that the aorta is ruptured and the patient is losing blood at the rate of a pint every minute, MYCIN will try to find a bacterial cause of the problem.

Thus, because we still perform all the abstractions for our programs, most AI work is still done in the blocks world. Now the blocks have slightly different shapes and colors, but their underlying semantics have not changed greatly.

It could be argued that performing this abstraction (perception) for AI programs is merely the normal reductionist use of abstraction common in all good science. The abstraction reduces the input data so that the program experiences the same perceptual world (*Merkwelt* in (Uexküll 1921)) as humans. Other (vision) researchers will independently fill in the details at some other time and place. I object to this on two grounds. First, as Uexküll and others have pointed out, each animal species, and clearly each robot species with their own distinctly non-human sensor suites, will have their own different *Merkwelt*. Second, the *Merkwelt* we humans provide our programs is based on our own introspection. It is by no means clear that such a *Merkwelt* is anything like what we actually use internally–it could just as easily be an output coding for communication purposes (e.g., most humans go through life never realizing, they have a large blind spot almost in the center of their visual fields).

The first objection warns of the danger that reasoning strategies developed for the human-assumed *Merkwelt* may not be valid when real sensors and perception processing is used. The second objection says that even with human sensors and perception the Merkwelt may not be anything like that used by humans. In fact, it may be the case that our introspective descriptions of our internal representations are completely misleading and quite different from what we really use.

3.1   A Continuing Story

Meanwhile our friends in the 1890s are busy at work on their AF machine. They have come to agree that the project is too big to be worked on as a single entity and that they will need to become specialists in different areas. After all, they had asked questions of fellow passengers on their flight and discovered that the Boeing Co. employed over 6000 people to build such an airplane.

Everyone is busy but there is not a lot of communication between the groups. The people making the passenger seats used the finest solid steel available as the framework. There was some muttering that perhaps they should use tubular steel to save weight, but the general consensus was that if such an obviously big and heavy airplane could fly then clearly there was no problem with weight.

On their observation flight none of the original group managed to get a glimpse of the driver's seat, but they have done some hard thinking and think they have established the major constraints on what should be there and how it should work. The pilot, as he will be called, sits in a seat above a glass floor so that he can see the ground below so he will know where to land. There are some side mirrors so he can watch behind for other approaching airplanes. His controls consist of a foot pedal to control speed (just as in these newfangled automobiles that are starting to appear), and a steering wheel to turn left and right. In addition, the wheel stem can be pushed forward and back to make the airplane go up and down. A clever arrangement of pipes measures airspeed of the airplane and displays it on a dial. What more could one want? Oh yes. There's a rather nice setup of louvers in the windows so that the driver can get fresh air without getting the full blast of the wind in his face.

An interesting sidelight is that all the researchers have by now abandoned the study of aerodynamics. Some of them had intensely questioned their fellow passengers on this subject and not one of the modern flyers had known a thing about it. Clearly the AF researchers had previously been wasting their time in its pursuit.

4   Incremental Intelligence

I wish to build completely autonomous mobile agents that co-exist in the world with humans, and are seen by those humans as intelligent beings in their own right. I will call such agents *Creatures*. This is my intellectual motivation. I have no particular interest in demonstrating how human beings work, although humans, like other animals, are interesting objects of study in this endeavor as they are successful autonomous agents. I have no particular interest in applications it seems clear to me that if my goals can be met then the range of applications for such Creatures will be limited only by our (or their) imagination. I have no particular interest in the philosophical implications of Creatures, although clearly there will be significant implications.

Given the caveats of the previous two sections and considering the parable of the AF researchers, I am convinced that I must tread carefully in this endeavor to avoid some nasty pitfalls.

For the moment then, consider the problem of building Creatures as an engineering problem. We will develop an *engineering methodology* for building Creatures.

First, let us consider some of the requirements for our Creatures.

- A Creature must cope appropriately and in a timely fashion with changes in its dynamic environment.

- A Creature should be robust with respect to its environment; minor changes in the properties of the world should not lead to total collapse of the Creature's behavior; rather one should expect only a gradual change in capabilities of the Creature as the environment changes more and more.

- A Creature should be able to maintain multiple goals and, depending on the circumstances it finds itself in, change which particular goals it is actively pursuing; thus it can both adapt to surroundings and capitalize on fortuitous circumstances.

- A Creature should do *something* in the world; it should have some purpose in being.

Now, let us consider some of the valid engineering approaches to achieving these requirements. As in all engineering endeavors it is necessary to decompose a complex system into parts, build the parts, then interface them into a complete system.

4.1 Decomposition by Function

Perhaps the strongest, traditional notion of intelligent systems (at least implicitly among AI workers) has been of a central system, with perceptual modules as inputs and action modules as outputs. The perceptual modules deliver a symbolic description of the world and the action modules take a symbolic description of desired actions and make sure they happen in the world. The central system then is a symbolic information processor.

Traditionally, work in perception (and vision is the most commonly studied form of perception) and work in central systems has been done by different researchers and even totally different research laboratories. Vision workers are not immune to earlier criticisms of AI workers. Most vision research is presented as a transformation from one image representation (e.g., a raw grey scale image) to another registered image (e.g., an edge image). Each group, AI and vision, makes assumptions about the shape of the symbolic interfaces. Hardly anyone has ever connected a vision system to an intelligent central system. Thus the assumptions independent researchers make are not forced to be realistic. There is a real danger from pressures to neatly circumscribe the particular piece of research being done.

The central system must also be decomposed into smaller pieces. We see subfields of artificial intelligence such as "knowledge representation," "learning," "planning," "qualitative reasoning," etc. The interfaces between these modules are also subject to intellectual abuse.

When researchers working on a particular module get to choose both the inputs and the outputs that specify the module requirements I believe there is little chance the work they do will fit into a complete intelligent system.

This bug in the functional decomposition approach is hard to fix. One needs a long chain of modules to connect perception to action. In order to test any of them they all must first be built. But until realistic modules are built it is highly unlikely that we can predict exactly what modules will be needed or what interfaces they will need.

4.2 Decomposition by Activity

An alternative decomposition makes no distinction between peripheral systems, such as vision, and central systems. Rather the fundamental slicing up of an intelligent system is in the orthogonal direction dividing it into *activity* producing subsystems. Each activity, or behavior producing system individually connect s sensing to action. We refer to an activity producing system as a *layer*. An activity is a pattern of interactions with the world. Another name for our activities might well be *skill*, emphasizing that each activity can at least post facto be rationalized as pursuing some purpose. We have chosen the word activity, however, because our layers must decide when to act for themselves, not be some subroutine to be invoked at the beck and call of some other layer.

The advantage of this approach is that it gives an incremental path from very simple systems to complex autonomous intelligent systems. At each step of the way it is only necessary to build one small piece, and interface it to an existing, working, complete intelligence.

The idea is to first build a very simple complete autonomous system, and *test it in the real world*. Our favourite example of such a system is a Creature, actually a mobile robot, which avoids hitting things. It senses objects in its immediate vicinity and moves away from them, halting if it senses something in its path. It is still necessary to build this system by decomposing it into parts, but there need be no clear distinction between a "perception subsystem," a "central system" and an "action system." In fact, there may well be two independent channels connecting sensing to action (one for initiating motion, and one for emergency halts), so there is no single place where "perception" delivers a representation of the world in the traditional sense.

Next we build an incremental layer of intelligence which operates in parallel to the first system. It is pasted on to the existing debugged system and tested again in the real world. This new layer might directly access the sensors and run a different algorithm on the delivered data. The first-level autonomous system continues to run in parallel, and unaware of the existence of the second level. For example, in (Brooks 1986) we reported on building a first layer of control which let the Creature avoid objects and then adding a layer which instilled an activity of trying to visit distant visible places. The second layer injected commands to the motor control part of the first layer directing the robot towards the goal, but independently the first layer would cause the robot to veer away from previously unseen obstacles. The second layer monitored the progress of the Creature and sent updated motor commands, thus achieving its goal without being explicitly aware of obstacles, which had been handled by the lower level of control.

5   Who Has the Representations?

With multiple layers, the notion of perception delivering a description of the world gets blurred even more as the part of the system doing perception is spread out over many pieces which are not particularly connected by data paths or related by function. Certainly there is no

identifiable place where the "output" of perception can be found. Furthermore, totally different sorts of processing of the sensor data proceed
independently and in parallel, each affecting the overall system activity
through quite different channels of control.

In fact, not by design, but rather by observation we note that a
common theme in the ways in which our layered and distributed approach helps our Creatures meet our goals is that there is no central
representation.

- Low-level simple activities can instill the Creature with reactions
  to dangerous or important changes in its environment. Without
  complex representations and the need to maintain those representations and reason about them, these reactions can easily be made
  quick enough to serve their purpose. The key idea is to sense
  the environment often, and so have an up-to-date idea of what is
  happening in the world.

- By having multiple parallel activities, and by removing the idea
  of a central representation, there is less chance that any given
  change in the class of properties enjoyed by the world can cause
  total collapse of the system. Rather one might expect that a given
  change will at most incapacitate some but not all of the levels of
  control. Gradually as a more alien world is entered (alien in the
  sense that the properties it holds are different from the properties
  of the world in which the individual layers were debugged), the
  performance of the Creature might continue to degrade. By not
  trying to have an analogous model of the world, centrally located in
  the system, we are less likely to have built in a dependence on that
  model being completely accurate. Rather, individual layers extract
  only those *aspects* (Agre & Chapman n.d.) of the world which
  they find relevant–projections of a representation into a simple
  subspace, if you like. Changes in the fundamental structure of
  the world have less chance of being reflected in every one of those
  projections than they would have of showing up as a difficulty in
  matching some query to a central single world model.

- Each layer of control can be thought of as having its own implicit purpose (or goal if you insist). Since they are *active* layers,
  running in parallel and with access to sensors, they can monitor
  the environment and decide on the appropriateness of their goals.
  Sometimes goals can be abandoned when circumstances seem un-
  promising, and other times fortuitous circumstances can be taken
  advantage of. The key idea here is to be using the world as its
  own model and to continuously match the preconditions of each

goal against the real world. Because there is separate hardware for
each layer we can match as many goals as can exist in parallel, and
do not pay any price for higher numbers of goals as we would if we
tried to add more and more sophistication to a single processor,
or even some multiprocessor with a capacity-bounded network.

- The purpose of the Creature is implicit in its higher-level purposes,
  goals or layers. There need be no explicit representation of goals
  that some central (or distributed) process selects from to decide
  what. is most appropriate for the Creature to do next.

5.1   No Representation versus No Central Representation

Just as there is no central representation there is not even a central
system. Each activity producing layer connects perception to action directly. It is only the observer of the Creature who imputes a central
representation or central control. The Creature itself has none; it is a
collection of competing behaviors. Out of the local chaos of their interactions there emerges, in the eye of an observer, a coherent pattern of
behavior. There is no central purposeful locus of control. Minsky (Minsky 1986) gives a similar account of how human behavior is generated.

Note carefully that we are not claiming that chaos is a necessary in-
gredient of intelligent behavior. Indeed, we advocate careful engineering
of all the interactions within the system (evolution had the luxury of
incredibly long time scales and enormous numbers of individual experiments and thus perhaps was able to do without this careful engineering).

We do claim however, that there need be no explicit representation
of either the world or the intentions of the system to generate intelligent behaviors for a Creature. Without such explicit representations,
and when viewed locally, the interactions may indeed seem chaotic and
without purpose.

I claim there is more than this, however. Even at a local, level we
do not have traditional AI representations. We never use tokens which
have any semantics that can be attached to them. The best that can be
said in our implementation is that one number is passed from a process
to another. But it is only by looking at the state of both the first and
second processes that that number can be given any interpretation at
all. An extremist might say that we really do have representations,
but that they are just implicit. With an appropriate mapping of the
complete system and its state to another domain, we could define a
representation that these numbers and topological connections between
processes somehow encode.

However we are not happy with calling such things a representation. They differ from standard representations in too many ways.

There are no variables (e.g., see (Agre & Chapman n.d.) for a more thorough treatment of this) that need instantiation in reasoning processes. There are no rules which need to be selected through pattern matching. There are no choices to be made. To a large extent the state of the world determines the action of the Creature. Simon (Simon 1969) noted that the complexity of behavior of a system was not necessarily inherent in the complexity of the creature, but Perhaps in the complexity of the environment. He made this analysis in his description of an Ant wandering the beach, but ignored its implications in the next paragraph when he talked about humans. We hypothesize (following Agre and Chapman) that much of even human level activity is similarly a reflection of the world through very simple mechanisms without detailed representations.

6 The Methodology, in Practice

In order to build systems based on an activity decomposition so that they are truly robust we must rigorously follow a careful methodology.

6.1 Methodological Maxims

First, it is vitally important to test the Creatures we build in the real world; i.e., in the same world that we humans inhabit. It is disastrous to fall into the temptation of testing them in a simplified world first, even with the best intentions of later transferring activity to an unsimplified world. With a simplified world (matte painted walls, rectangular vertices everywhere, colored blocks as the only obstacles) it is very easy to accidentally build a submodule of the system which happens to rely on some of those simplified properties. This reliance can then easily be reflected in the requirements on the interfaces between that submodule and others. The disease spreads and the complete system depends in a subtle way on the simplified world. When it comes time to move to the, unsimplified world, we gradually and painfully realize that every piece of the system must be rebuilt. Worse than that we may need to rethink the total design as the issues may change completely. We are not so concerned that it might be dangerous to test simplified Creatures first and later add more sophisticated layers of control because evolution has been successful using this approach.

Second, as each layer is built it must be tested extensively in the real world. The system must interact with the real world over extended periods. Its behavior must be observed and be carefully and thoroughly debugged. When a second layer is added to an existing layer there are three potential sources of bugs: the first layer, the second layer, or the interaction of the two layers. Eliminating the first of these source of bugs as a possibility makes finding bugs much easier. Furthermore, there is only one thing possible to vary in order to fix the bugs–the second layer.

6.2   An Instantiation of the Methodology

We have built a series of four robots based on the methodology of task decomposition. They all operate in an unconstrained dynamic world (laboratory and office areas in the MIT Artificial Intelligence Laboratory). They successfully operate with people walking by, people deliberately trying to confuse them, and people just standing by watching them. All four robots are Creatures in the sense that on power-up they exist in the world and interact with it, pursuing multiple goals determined by their control layers implementing different activities. This is in contrast to other mobile robots that are given programs or plans to follow for a specific mission,

The four robots are shown in Figure 1. Two are identical, so there are really three, designs. One uses an offboard LISP machine for most of its computations, two use onboard combinational networks, and one uses a custom onboard parallel processor. All the robots implement the same abstract architecture, which we call the *subsumption architecture* which embodies the fundamental ideas of decomposition into layers of task achieving behaviors, and incremental composition through debugging in the real world. Details of these implementations can be found in (Brooks 1986).

Each layer in the subsumption architecture is composed of a fixed-topology network of simple finite state machines. Each finite state machine has a handful of states, one or two internal registers, one or two internal timers, and access to simple computational machines, which can compute things such as vector sums. The finite state machines run asynchronously, sending and receiving fixed length messages (1-bit messages on the two small robots, and 24-bit messages on the larger ones) over *wires*. On our first robot these were virtual wires; on our later robots we have used physical wires to connect computational components.

There is no central locus of control. Rather, the finite state machines are data-driven by the messages they receive. The arrival of messages or the expiration of designated time periods cause the finite state machines to change state. The finite state machines have access to the contents of the messages and might output them, test them with a predicate and conditionally branch to a different state, or pass them to simple computation elements. There is no possibility of access to global data,

Figure 1: The four MIT AI laboratory "Mobots." Left-most is the first built Allen, which relies on an offboard LISP machine for computation support. The right-most one is Herbert, shown with a 24 node CMOS parallel processor surrounding its girth. New sensors and fast early vision processors are still to be built and installed. In the middle are Tom and Jerry, based on a commercial toy chassis, with single PALs (Programmable Array of Logic) as their controllers.

nor of dynamically established communications links. There is thus no possibility of global control. All finite state machines are equal, yet at the same time they are prisoners of their fixed topology connections.

Layers are combined through mechanisms we call *suppression* (whence the name subsumption architecture) and *inhibition*. In both cases as a new layer is added, one of the new wires is side-tapped into an existing wire. A pre-defined time constant is associated with each side-tap. In the case of suppression the side-tapping occurs on the input side of a finite state machine. If a message arrives on the net wire it is directed to the input port of the finite state machine as though it had arrived on the existing wire. Additionally, any new messages on the existing wire are suppressed (i.e., rejected) for the specified time period. For inhibition the side-tapping occurs on the output side of a finite state machine. A message on the new wire simply inhibits messages being emitted on the existing wire for the specified time period. Unlike suppression the new message is not delivered in their place.

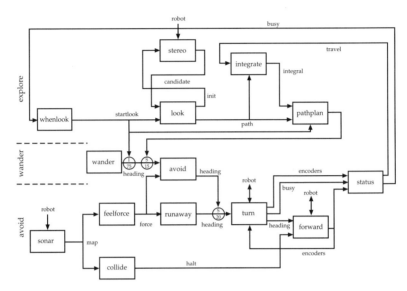

Figure 2: We wire, finite state machines together into layers of control. Each layer is built on top of existing layers. Lower level layers never rely on the existence of higher level layers.

As an example, consider the three layers of Figure 2. These are three layers of control that we have run on our first mobile robot for well over a year. The robot has a ring of twelve ultrasonic sonars as its primary sensors. Every second these sonars are run to give twelve radial depth measurements. Sonar is extremely noisy due to many objects being mirrors to sonar. There are thus problems with specular reflection and return paths following multiple reflections due to surface skimming with low angles of incidence (less than thirty degrees). In more detail the three layers work as follows:

1. The lowest-level layer implements a behavior which makes the robot (the physical embodiment of the Creature) avoid hitting objects. It both avoids static objects and moving objects, even those that are actively attacking it. The finite state machine labelled *sonar* simply runs the sonar devices and every second emits an instantaneous map with the readings converted to polar coordinates. This map is passed on to the *collide* and *feelforce* finite state machine. The first of these simply watches to see if there is anything dead ahead, and if so sends a *halt* message to the finite state machine in charge of running the robot forwards–if that finite state machine is not in the correct state the message may well be ignored. Simultaneously, the other finite state machine computes a repulsive force on the robot, based on an inverse square law, where each sonar return is considered to indicate the presence of a repulsive object. The contributions from each sonar are added to produce an overall force acting on the robot. The output is passed to the *runaway* machine which thresholds it and passes it on to the *turn* machine which orients the robot directly away from the summed repulsive force. Finally, the *forward* machine drives the robot forward. Whenever this machine receives a halt message while the robot is driving forward, it commands the robot to halt.

This network of finite state machines generates behaviors which let the robot avoid objects. If it starts in the middle of an empty room it simply sits there. If someone walks up to it, the robot moves away. If it moves in the direction of other obstacles it halts. Overall, it manages to exist in a dynamic environment without hitting or being hit by objects. **2.** The next layer makes the robot wander about, when not busy avoiding objects. The *wander* finite state machine generates a random heading for the robot every ten seconds or so. The *avoid* machine treats that heading as an attractive force and sums it with the repulsive force computed from the sonars. It uses the result to suppress the lower-level behavior, forcing the robot to move in a direction close to what *wander* decided but at the same time avoid any obstacles. Note that if the *turn* and *forward* finite state machines are busy running the robot the new impulse to wander will be ignored. **3.** The third layer makes the robot try to explore. It looks for distant places, then tries to reach them. This layer suppresses the wander layer, and observes how the bottom layer diverts the robot due to obstacles, (perhaps dynamic). It corrects for any divergences and the robot achieves the goal.

The *whenlook* finite state machine notices when the robot is not busy moving, and starts up, the free space finder (labelled stereo in the diagram) finite state machine. At the same time it inhibits wandering behavior so that the observation will remain valid. When a path is observed it is sent to the *pathplan* finite state machine, which injects a commanded direction to the *avoid* finite state machine. In this way, lower-level obstacle avoidance continues to function. This may cause the robot to go in a direction different to that desired by *pathplan*. For that reason the actual path of the robot is monitored by the *integrate* finite state machine, which sends updated estimates to the *pathplan* machine. This machine then acts as a difference engine forcing the robot in the desired direction and compensating for the actual path of the robot as it avoids obstacles.

These particular layers were implemented on our first robot. See (Brooks 1986) for more details. Brooks and Connell (Brooks & Connell

1986) report on another three layers implemented on that particular robot.

7   What This Is Not

The subsumption architecture with its network of simple machines is reminiscent, at the surface level at least, with a number of mechanistic approaches to intelligence, such as connectionism and neural networks. But it is different in many respects for these endeavors, and also quite different from many other post-Dartmouth traditions in artificial intelligence. We very briefly explain those differences in the following sections.

7.1   It Isn't Connectionism

Connectionists try to make networks of simple processors. In that regard, the things they build (in simulation only–no connectionist has ever driven a real robot in a real environment, no matter how simple) are similar to the subsumption networks we build. However, their processing nodes tend to be uniform and they are looking (as their name suggests) for revelations from understanding how to connect them correctly (which is usually assumed to mean richly at least). Our nodes are all unique finite state machines and the density of connections is very much lower, certainly not uniform, and very low indeed between layers. Additionally, connectionists seem to be looking for explicit distributed representations to spontaneously arise from their networks. We harbor no such hopes because we believe representations are not necessary and appear only in the eye or mind of the observer.

7.2   It Isn't Neural Networks

Neural networks is the parent discipline of which connectionism is a recent incarnation. Workers in neural networks claim that there is some biological significance to their network nodes, as models of neurons. Most of the, models seem wildly implausible given the paucity of modeled connections relative to the thousands found in real neurons. We claim no biological significance in our choice of finite state machines as network nodes.

7.3   It Isn't Production Rules

Each individual activity producing layer of our architecture could be viewed as an implementation of a production rule. When the right conditions are met in the environment a certain action will be performed.

We feel that analogy is a little like saying that any FORTRAN program with IF statements is implementing a production rule system. A standard production system really is more–it has a rule base, from which a rule is selected based on matching preconditions of all the rules to some database. The preconditions may include variables which must be matched to individuals in the database, but layers run in parallel and have no variables or need for matching. Instead, aspects of the world are extracted and these directly trigger or modify certain behaviors of the layer.

7.4   It Isn't a Blackboard

If one, really wanted, one could make an analogy of our networks to a blackboard, control architecture. Some of the finite state machines would be localized knowledge sources. Others would be processes acting on these knowledge sources by finding them on the blackboard. There is a simplifying point in our, architecture however: all the processes know exactly where to look on the blackboard as they are hard-wired to the correct place. I think this forced analogy indicates its own weakness. There is no flexibility at all on where a process can gather appropriate knowledge. Most advanced blackboard architectures make heavy use of the general sharing and availability of almost all knowledge. Furthermore, in spirit at least, blackboard systems tend to hide from a consumer of knowledge who the particular producer was. This is the primary means of abstraction in blackboard systems. In our system we make such connections explicit and permanent.

7.5   It Isn't German Philosophy

In some circles much credence is given to Heidegger as one who understood the dynamics of existence. Our approach has certain similarities to work inspired by this German philosopher (e.g., (Agre & Chapman n.d.)) but our work was not so inspired. It is based purely on engineering considerations. That does not preclude it from being used in philosophical debate as an example on any side of any fence, however.

8   Limits to Growth

Since our approach is a performance-based one, it is the performance of the systems we build which must be used to measure its usefulness and to point to its limitations.

We claim that as of mid-1987 our robots, using the subsumption architecture to implement complete Creatures, are the most reactive real-time mobile robots in existence. Most other mobile robots are still at the stage of individual "experimental runs" in static environments, or at best in completely mapped static environments. Ours, on the other hand, operate completely autonomously in complex dynamic environments at the flick of their on switches, and continue until their batteries are drained. We believe they operate at a level closer to simple insect level intelligence than to bacteria level intelligence. Our goal (worth nothing if we don't deliver) is simple insect level intelligence within two years. Evolution took 3 billion years to get from single cells to insects, and only another 500 million years from there to humans. This statement is not intended as a prediction of our future performance, but rather to indicate the nontrivial nature of insect level intelligence.

Despite this good performance to date, there are a number of serious questions about our approach. We have beliefs and hopes about how these questions will be resolved, but under our criteria only performance truly counts. Experiments and building more complex systems take time, so with the caveat that the experiments described below have not yet been performed we outline how we currently see our endeavor progressing. Our intent in discussing this is to indicate that there is at least a plausible path forward to more intelligent machines from our current situation.

Our belief is that the sorts of activity producing layers of control we are developing (mobility, vision and survival related tasks) are necessary prerequisites for higher-level intelligence in the style we attribute to human beings.

The most natural and serious questions concerning limits of our approach are:

- How many layers can be built in the subsumption architecture before the interactions between layers become too complex to continue?

- How complex can the behaviors be that are developed without the aid of central representations?

- Can higher-level functions such as learning occur in these fixed topology networks of simple finite state machines?

We outline our current thoughts on these questions.

8.1   How Many Layers?

The highest number of layers we have run on a physical robot is three. In simulation we have run six parallel layers. The technique of completely

debugging the robot on all existing activity producing layers before designing and adding a new one seems to have been practical till now at
least.

8.2   How Complex?

We are currently working towards a complex behavior pattern on our
fourth robot which will require approximately fourteen individual activity producing layers.

The robot has infrared proximity sensors for local obstacle avoidance.
It has an onboard manipulator which can grasp objects at ground and
table-top levels, and also determine their rough weight. The hand has
depth sensors mounted on it so that homing in on a target object in
order to grasp it can be controlled directly. We are currently working on
a structured light laser scanner to determine rough depth maps in the
forward looking direction from the robot.

The high-level behavior we are trying to instill in this Creature is to
wander around the office areas of our laboratory, find open office doors,
enter, retrieve empty soda cans from cluttered desks in crowded offices
and return them to a central repository.

In order to achieve this overall behavior a number of simpler task
achieving behaviors are necessary They include: avoiding objects, following walls, recognizing doorways and going through them, aligning on
learned landmarks, heading in a homeward direction, learning homeward
bearings at landmarks and following them, locating table-like objects,
approaching such objects, scanning table tops for cylindrical objects of
roughly the height of a soda can, serving the manipulator arm, moving
the hand above sensed objects, using the hand sensor to look for objects
of soda can size sticking up from a background, grasping objects if they
are light enough, and depositing objects.

The individual tasks need not be coordinated by any central controller. Instead they can index off of the state of the world. For instance
the grasp behavior can cause the manipulator to grasp any object of the
appropriate size seen by the hand sensors. The robot will not randomly
grasp just any object however, because it will only be when other layers
or behaviors have noticed an object of roughly the right shape on top
of a table-like object that the grasping behavior will find itself in a position where its sensing of the world tells it to react. If, from above, the
object no longer looks like a soda can, the grasp reflex will not happen
and other lower-level behaviors will cause the robot to look elsewhere
for new candidates.

8.3   Is Learning and Such Possible?

Some insects demonstrate a simple type of learning that has been dubbed "learning by instinct" (Gould & Marler 1986). It is hypothesized that honey bees for example are pre-wired to learn how to. distinguish certain classes of flowers, and to learn routes to and from a home hive and sources of nectar. Other insects, butterflies, have been shown to be able to learn to distinguish flowers, but in an information limited way (Lewis 1986). If they are forced to learn about a second sort of flower, they forget what they already knew about the first, in a manner that suggests the total amount of information which they know, remains constant.

We have found a way to build fixed topology networks of our finite state machines which can perform learning, as an isolated subsystem, at levels comparable to these examples. At the moment of course we are in the very position we lambasted most AI workers for earlier in this paper. We have an isolated module of a system working, and the inputs and outputs have been left dangling.

We are working to remedy this situation, but experimental work with physical Creatures is a nontrivial and time consuming activity. We find that almost any pre-designed piece of equipment or software has so many preconceptions of how they are to be used built into them, that they are not flexible enough to be a part of our complete systems. Thus, as of mid-1987, our work in learning is held up by the need to build a new sort of video camera and high-speed low-power processing box to run specially developed vision algorithms at 10 frames per second. Each of these steps is a significant engineering endeavor which we are undertaking as fast as resources permit.

Of course, talk is cheap.

8.4   The Future

Only experiments with real Creatures in real worlds can answer the natural doubts about our approach. Time will tell.

Acknowledgements

Phil Agre, David Chapman, Peter Cudhea, Anita Flynn, David Kirsh and Thomas Marill made many helpful comments on earlier drafts of this paper.

This report describes research done at the Artificial Intelligence Laboratory of the Massachusetts Institute of Technology. Support for the research is provided in part by an IBM Faculty 9 Development Award, in part by a grant from the Systems Development Foundation, in part by the University Research Initiative under Office of Naval Research contract N00014-86-K-0685 and in part by the Advanced Research Projects Agency under Office of Naval Research contract N00014-85-K-0124.

CHAPTER 6

....

PLANNING IS JUST A WAY OF AVOIDING FIGURING OUT WHAT TO DO NEXT

This was a short paper I wrote to answer the criticism of behavior-based robotics that there was no place for having plans. Somehow plans were so central a notion to classical Artificial Intelligence at the time that this criticism was always used as a trump to argue that the approach could go nowhere. In this paper I argued that the notion of a plan was, like cognition as discussed in the preface, at best something that human observers attributed to a system. Actually concretizing a plan in a robot was simply an exercise that gets in the way of the robot being effective. This is a continuation of the argument that the intelligent control of systems needed to be sliced up a different way from the conventional viewpoint. Plans need not exist explicitly. Rather they are a descriptive property of a system constructed in a fundamentally different way.

Abstract. The idea of planning and plan execution is just an intuition based decomposition. There is no reason it *has to be* that way. Most likely in the long term, real empirical evidence from systems we **know** to be built that way (from designing them like that) will determine whether its a very good idea or not. Any particular planner is simply an abstraction barrier. Below that level we get a choice of whether to slot in another planner or to place a program which *does the right thing*. Why stop there? Maybe we can go up the hierarchy and eliminate the planners there too. To do this we must move from a state based way of reasoning to a process based way of acting.

McDermott (1987) recently asked the following questions in regard to the need to do resarch in interleaving planning and run-time monitoring of senors:

Originally appeared as MIT Artificial Intelligence Laboratory *Working Paper 303*, September, 1987.

Are sensors good enough yet for us to be thinking about how to reason about their inputs? Is planning research just a typical AI moonshine enterprise, thinking about hypothetical scenarios that don't resemble what will actually be possible once high-quality sensors are available? We can distinguish three positions on this question:

Theism: Execution monitoring is important enough, and the issues clear enough, for us to be thinking about them right now.

Atheism: The whole idea of plan execution and the run-time maintenance of something called a "plan" is misguided. Controlling the behavior of a robot is a matter of putting sensors and effectors together using a program.

Agnosticism: We won't be able to settle the issue until much better sensor technology is available.

This is my reply to McDermott.

I am an atheist in McDermott's sense:

An atheist usually has very little hope of convincing a theist of his folly. The theist afterall has his own self consistent set of beliefs. Likewise I expect to make little progress arguing with planning theists. I expect they will make little progress arguing with me.

But religous theists and atheists have an extra problem to deal with. The only possible resolution of the debate involves one of the participants dying, and even then at most one of them learns the true facts. In the matter of plan execution, however, we have an empirical test available! We can try to build real robots that operate in real environments and see which ones work better and appear more intelligent; those with traditional AI planning and execution monitoring systems or those with reflexive or subsumption architectures. One of us will have to eat our words!

But will this happen soon; aren't our computers too small yet? Heck no. Part of my thesis is that it actually takes very little computational power; we've just been organizing it all wrong up until now.

1   Wrong Decomposition

I'll start with some seemingly irrelevant fables. However, I do believe they are precisely relevant and applicable to the debate about planning and execution.

1.1 Fable 1: How Does a FORTRAN Computer Work?

Once upon a time in a land far away a young boy was given a book on FORTRAN programming. The boy had never seen a real computer, nor had any idea how one worked or what it really did, but he had seen pictures of "giant brains" in '50s juvenile science books along with a discussion of binary arithmetic, and simple relay-based switching circuits.

He started reading the FORTRAN book and was immediately convinced of the power of computers. He wanted to program one. And he started thinking about how one might be built.

It was pretty clear how to break the problem down into functional units. There must be a method of encoding the characters on the FORTRAN coding sheets into binary numbers which then control the switching paths in the rest of the computer. There also must be a big set of memory registers (he thought of them as little cubby holes that you could put numbers in). One sort for **REAL** numbers (about twenty twenty-sixths of them) and one sort for **INTEGER** numbers (the other six twenty-sixths). Actually there must be a lot of these registers; one named **A**, one named **B**, one named **XYZZY**, one name **B365QL**, etc. In fact there must be $26 \times 36 \times 36 \times 36 \times 36 \times 36$ of them. He never bothered to multiply it out, but, gee, there's an awful lot of them. Maybe thats why computers cost over a million dollars (and remember this is when a million dollars was real money!). Oh, and then there must be a set of circuits to do arithmetic (pretty easy to see how to do that) and a way of getting numbers back and forth to the cubbyholes.

So that was how to build a computer. Then the boy read the chapter on arrays and did a few multiplications with pencil and paper. Oh, oh!

1.2 Fable 2: OK, How Does a FORTRAN Computer Really Work?

In another universe some neuroscientists were given a FORTRAN computer. They wanted to figure out how it worked. They knew that in running a porgram there were three different processes: compilation, linking and loading. They decided to first isolate in the machine, subareas where each of these things were done. Then they'd be able to study each of them in isolation and in more detail. So they got some oscilloscopes and started probing the wires and solder points within the machine as it ran programs, trying to correlate the signal trains with what the operator console reported was happening.

They tried for many years but activity throughout most of the circuits from a global perspective seemed uniformly like white noise. Locally they could establish correlations, but not correlate that with what the console reported. The only susbstantial clue was that a rotating mechanical device made a different pattern of noises when the different computer behaviors were dominant. One popular hypothesis was that all the real computing was done mechanically in thus unit somehow and that all the electrical circuits where just a routing network to get stuff to and from the I/O devices. But there were other hypotheses too. Maybe the computer was using holograms.

1.3   The Point

The point of these fables is that without having designed a device your-self, or thought through a design completely, you may very well make completely the wrong functional decomposition by simply observing its behavior. The same is true of observing human behavior. Ethologists have discovered this in observing insects and lower animals. Early and folk or intuitive explanations of what the creature is doing have had to undergo radical change when more careful observation and experiment with the total system (creature and environment) have been carried out.

The idea of planning and plan execution is just an intuition based decomposition. It may well be the wrong decomposition. There may be no reason it *has to be* that way. All we have to go on is our intuition of how we work—historically that intuition has been wrong. Most likely in the long term, real empirical evidence from systems we **know** to be built with planners and plan execution modules (from designing them like that) will determine whether its a very good idea or not.

2   What's Wrong with Models and Plans?

Plans provide a useful level of abstraction for a designer or observer of a system but provide nothing to a robot operationally.

If you allow the notion of explicit plans for a robot you run into a problem of which level of abstraction should the plan be described at. Whatever you decide, upon examination it will turn out to be a bogus and arbitrary decision.

2.1   How Much Detail?

Consider a mobile robot which must cross from one part of a room to another. A traditional AI planner would ignore the geometry of the room and simply have a list of known named places and would issue some plan step like *MOVE from A to B*. Then it is up to some assumed runtime system to execute this step, and perhaps re-invoke the planner if

it fails for some reason. In simulation systems the runtime system typically achieves such plan steps atomically. But when many AI-roboticists
came to implement the runtime systems on physical robots they found
they needed to use a planner also (e.g., (Moravec 1983)). This planner
takes into account a floor plan modelled from sensor data and plans a
collision free path for the robot (and usually it is only intended for static
environments, not those with people moving about in them). Some such
robots then send the individual path segments off to subroutines which
execute them. Others rely on yet another level of explicit planning to
decide on how to accelerate the motors, perhaps based on a model of
the mechanical dynamics of the vehicle. All such planners that I know
of then pass a series of commands off to some lower level program which
does the right thing; i.e., it takes the action specification and directly
translates it into signals to drive motors. One could imagine however,
yet another level of planning, where an explicit model of the drive circuits was used to symbolically plan how to vary the motor currents and
voltages!

We thus see that any particular planner is simply an abstraction
barrier. Below that level we get a choice of whether to slot in another
planner or to place a program which *does the right thing*. What could
this mean? Let's look at some examples from robotics.

2.2   Previous Examples from Robotics

Below are two pertinent examples from robotics. In both cases early
attempts to control a robot by telling it how to set its joints in space
have been replaced by telling it the parameters to use in tight feedback
loops with its environment. The controlling program no longer tells it,
nor knows, nor cares, where to set its joints. Rather, in each case, the
robot acts differentially to the environment, trying to maintain set points
in a higher order space. As a result of interaction with the environment
the overall goal is achieved without the robot controller ever knowing
the complete details of how it was done.

In the early days of research robotics, and even today in most of
industry it was assumed that the right abstraction level for talking to a
manipulator robot was to tell it to go someplace. The driver program,
or planner perhaps, sends down a series of desired locations and orien-
tations for the end effector (some systems operate in joint coordinates,
while others operate in cartesian coordinates). This is known as *position
control*.

Experience over many years has shown some problems with this approach. First, in order to interact well with the world, the world model
must have extremely high precision; making sensing difficult and expen-

sive. Second, in order to carry out tasks with low error tolerances, it is necessary to have precise position control over the robot; clearly making it more expensive. But since position accuracy is critically dependent on the available dynamic model of the robot and since grasping a payload alters the manipulator dynamics we have seen a trend towards more and more massive robots carrying smaller and smaller payloads. Manipulator to payload mass ratios of 100 to 1 are almost the rule and ratios of 1000 to 1 are not unheard of. Compare this to the human arm.

Recently researchers have realized that position control was not the best way to approach the problem. Now research abounds on *force control* and ways to use it (automatically) to achieve delicate and precise goals. The major idea in force control is that rather than tell the robot to achieve some *position* it is instead told to achieve some *force* in its interaction with the environment. As long as the desired force is appropriate for the circumstances, the physical interaction of the robot and the world guide it to achieving some desired goal. For instance holding a peg tilted at an angle and applying a force outside the friction (or sticking) cone, the peg slides across a surface until the lowest corner drops into a tight fitting hole, whereafter the peg slides down the hole. Much tighter tolerance assemblies can be achieved in this way than with the use of pure position control. Indeed many of the force control strategies used tend to be similar to those used by humans.

Notice that at no time does any program have to know or care precisely where the robot will be. Rather a "planner" must arrange things so that the constraints from the physical world are exactly right so that the robot, operating so as to do the specified right thing, can't but help achieve the higher level goal. The trick is to find a process for the robot which is stable in achieving the goal over a wide range of initial conditions and applied forces. Then the world need not be modelled so precisely and the manipulator dynamics need not be known so precisely.

In a second example of this trend, Raibert, Brown & Murthy (1984) has elegantly demonstrated that the intuitive decomposition of how to walk or run is maybe not the best. Most previous work in walking machines had concentrated on maintaining static stability and carefully planning where and when to move each leg and foot. Raibert instead decomposed the running problem for a one (and later two and four) legged robot into one of separately maintaining hopping height, forward velocity and body attitude. There is certainly no notion of planning how the running robot will move its joints, where exactly the foot will be placed in an absolute coordinate system, or where the body will be in six dimensional configuration space at any give time. These questions do not even make sense within the decomposition Raibert has developed.

Both these are example of redefining the *right thing* is in a way that radically redefines the "planning" problem.

2.3 What Does This All Mean?

Brooks (1986) has shown that there is another way to implement *MOVE from A to B*.[1] A simple difference engine forces the robot to move towards *B* while other parallel activities take care of avoiding obstacles (even dynamic ones). Essentially the idea is to set up appropriate, well conditioned, tight feedback loops between sensing and action, with the external world as the medium for the loop.

So it looks like we can get rid of all the planners that normally exist below a traditional AI planner. Why stop there? Maybe we can go up the hierarchy and eliminate the planners there too. But how can we do this?

We need to move away from state as the primary abstraction for thinking about the world. Rather we should think about processes which implement the *right thing*. We arrange for certain processes to be predisposed to be active and then given the right physical circumstances the goal will be achieved. The behaviors are gated on sensory inputs and so are only active under circumstances where they might be appropriate. Of course, one needs to have a number of pre-disposed behaviors to provide robustness when the primary behavior fails due to being gated out.

As we keep finding out what sort of processes implement the *right thing*, we continually redefine what the planner is expected to do. Eventually we won't need one.

3 Simulation

McDermott (1987) also asks whether it is sufficient to pursue these questions using simulated systems. The answer is a clear no.

I support the use of simulation as an adjunct to real world experiments. It can cut development time and point up problems before expensive hardware is built. However it requires a constant feedback from real experiments to ensure that it is not being abused.

The basic problem is that simulation is a very dangerous weapon indeed. It is full of temptations to be mis-used. At any level there is a temptation to over idealize just what the sensors can deliver. Worse, the user may make a genuine mistake, not realizing just how much noise

---

[1] Although his work suggests that this is not an appropriate subgoal to be considered for a higher level plan.

exists in the real world. Even worse than that however, is the temptation to simulate the 'perception' system. Now we jump right into making up a decomposition and stating requirements on what the perception system will deliver. Typically it is supposed to deliver the identity and location of objects. There exists no computer perception system today that can do such a thing except under very controlled circumstances (e.g., a small library of machined parts can be localized and recognized in a small field of view from a fixed camera). I don't believe a general such system is even possible; for instance I don't believe humans have such a perception system. The idea that it is possible is based on the wrong-headed decomposition that gives us planning systems.

Don't use simulation as your primary testbed. In the long run you will be wasting your time and your sponsor's money.

CHAPTER 7

· ·

ELEPHANTS DON'T PLAY CHESS

By 1990 the criticisms of the behavior-based approach had taken on a rear guard flavor criticizing the approach for what it had not achieved. I felt that such arguments were unfair on two grounds. Firstly, it was not expected of other systems they that be able to do everything for everyone—chess playing programs were not criticized for not being able to do symbolic mathematics or assemble parts in a factory, nor were elephants criticized for not being able to play chess. Secondly, it seemed to me that the behavior-based robotic systems had done just as much and indeed much more than robotics systems based on conventional Artificial Intelligence. This paper tried to lay out some of that ground, and bring people up to date on what had been achieved.

Abstract. There is an alternative route to Artificial Intelligence that diverges from the directions pursued under that banner for the last thirty some years. The traditional approach has emphasized the abstract manipulation of symbols, whose grounding in physical reality has rarely been achieved. We explore a research methodology which emphasizes ongoing physical interaction with the environment as the primary source of constraint on the design of intelligent systems. We show how this methodology has recently had significant successes on a par with the most successful classical efforts. We outline plausible future work along these lines which can lead to vastly more ambitious systems.

1 Introduction

Artificial Intelligence research has foundered in a sea of incrementalism. No one is quite sure where to go save improving on earlier demonstrations of techniques in symbolic manipulation of ungrounded representations. At the same time, small AI companies are folding, and attendance is well

Originally appeared in *Robotics and Autonomous Systems 6*, 1990, pp. 3-15.

down at national and international Artificial Intelligence conferences. While it is true that the use of AI is prospering in many large companies, it is primarily through the application to novel domains of long developed techniques that have become passé in the research community.

What has gone wrong? (And how is this book the answer?!!)

In this paper we argue that the *symbol system hypothesis* upon which *classical AI* is based is fundamentally flawed, and as such imposes severe limitations on the fitness of its progeny. Further, we argue that the dogma of the symbol system hypothesis implicitly includes a number of largely unfounded great leaps of faith when called upon to provide a plausible path to the digital equivalent of human level intelligence. It is the chasms to be crossed by these leaps which now impede classical AI research.

But there is an alternative view, or dogma, variously called *nouvelle AI, fundamentalist AI*, or in a weaker form *situated activity*.[1] It is based on the *physical grounding hypothesis*. It provides a different methodology for building intelligent systems than that pursued for the last thirty years. The traditional methodology bases its decomposition of intelligence into functional information processing modules whose combinations provide overall system behavior. The new methodology bases its decomposition of intelligence into individual behavior generating modules, whose coexistence and co-operation let more complex behaviors emerge.

In classical AI, none of the modules themselves generate the behavior of the total system. Indeed it is necessary to combine together many of the modules to get any behavior at all from the system. Improvement in the competence of the system proceeds by improving the individual functional modules. In nouvelle AI each module itself generates behavior, and improvement in the competence of the system proceeds by adding new modules to the system.

Given that neither classical nor nouvelle AI seem close to revealing the secrets of the holy grail of AI, namely general purpose human level intelligence equivalence, there are a number of critical comparisons that can be made between the two approaches.

- Is either approach epistemologically adequate? (And adequate for what?)

- Are there clear paths for either approach in the direction of vastly more intelligent systems?

---

[1] Note that what is discussed in this paper is completely unrelated to what is popularly known as *Neural Networks* That given, there are nevertheless a number of aspects of nouvelle AI approaches which may be of interest to people working in classical neuroscience.

- Are nouvellers romantically hoping for magic from nothing while classicists are willing to tell their systems almost anything and everything, in the hope of teasing out the shallowest of inferences.

- Is the claim of emergent properties of nouvelle AI systems any more outrageous than the use of heuristics in classical AI?

In the following sections we address these issues.

2   The Symbol System Hypothesis

The symbol system hypothesis, (Simon 1969), states that intelligence operates on a system of symbols. The implicit idea is that perception and motor interfaces are sets of symbols on which the central intelligence system operates. Thus, the central system, or reasoning engine, operates in a domain independent way on the symbols. Their meanings are unimportant to the reasoner, but the coherence of the complete process emerges when an observer of the system knows the groundings of the symbols within his or her own experience.

Somewhat more implicitly in the work that the symbol system hypothesis has inspired, the symbols represent entities in the world. They may be individual objects, properties, concepts, desires, emotions, nations, colors, libraries, or molecules, but they are necessarily named entities. There are a number of effects which result from this commitment.

Recall first, however, that an intelligent system, apart from those which are experiments in the laboratory, will be embedded in the world in some form or another.

2.1   The Interface between Perception and Symbols

The central intelligence system deals in symbols. It must be fed symbols by the perception system.

But what is the correct symbolic description of the world around the intelligence system? Surely that description must be task dependent.

The default assumption has been that the perception system delivers a description of the world in terms of typed, named individuals and their relationships. For instance in the classic monkeys and bananas problem, the world description is in terms of boxes, bananas, and aboveness.

But for another task (e.g., deciding whether the bananas are rotten) quite a different representation might be important. Psychophysical evidence (Yarbus 1967) certainly points to perception being an active and task dependent operation.

The effect of the symbol system hypothesis has been to encourage vision researchers to quest after the goal of a general purpose vision system which delivers complete descriptions of the world in a symbolic form (e.g., Brooks (1981)). Only recently has there been a movement towards active vision (Ballard 1989) which is much more task dependent, or task driven (Agre & Chapman 1987).

2.2   Inadequacy of Simple Symbols

Symbol systems in their purest forms assume a knowable objective truth. It is only with much complexity that modal logics, or non-monotonic logics, can be built which better enable a system to have beliefs gleaned from partial views of a chaotic world.

As these enhancements are made, the realization of computations based on these formal systems becomes more and more biologically implausible. But once the commitment to symbol systems has been made it is imperative to push on through more and more complex and cumbersome systems in pursuit of objectivity.

This same pursuit leads to the well known frame problem (e.g., Pylyshyn (1987)), where it is impossible to assume anything that is not explicitly stated. Technical deviations around this problem have been suggested but they are by no means without their own problems.

2.3   Symbol Systems Rely on Emergent Properties

In general the reasoning process becomes trivial in an NP–complete space (e.g., Chapman (1987)). There have been large efforts to overcome these problems by choosing simple arithmetically computed *evaluation functions* or *polynomials* to guide the search. Charmingly, it has been hoped that intelligence will somehow emerge from these simple numeric computations carried out in the sea of symbols. Samuel (1959) was one of the earliest examples of this hope, which later turned out to be only partially correct (his learned polynomials later turned out to be dominated by piece count), but in fact almost all instances of search in classical AI have relied on such judiciously chosen polynomials to keep the search space manageable.

3   The Physical Grounding Hypothesis

Nouvelle AI is based on the physical grounding hypothesis. This hypothesis states that to build a system that is intelligent it is necessary to have its representations grounded in the physical world. Our experience with this approach is that once this commitment is made, the need for traditional symbolic representations soon fades entirely. The key observation is that the world is its own best model. It is always exactly up to date. It always contains every detail there is to be known. The trick is to sense it appropriately and often enough.

To build a system based on the physical grounding hypothesis it is necessary to connect it to the world via a set of sensors and actuators. Typed input and output are no longer of interest. They are not physically grounded.

Accepting the physical grounding hypothesis as a basis for research entails building systems in a bottom up manner. High level abstractions have to be made concrete. The constructed system eventually has to express all its goals and desires as physical action, and must extract all its knowledge from physical sensors. Thus the designer of the system is forced to make everything explicit. Every short-cut taken has a direct impact upon system competence, as there is no slack in the input/output representations. The forms of the low-level interfaces have consequences which ripple through the entire system.

3.1   Evolution

We already have an existence proof of the possibility of intelligent entities – human beings. Additionally many animals are intelligent to some degree. (This is a subject of intense debate, much of which really centers around a definition of intelligence.) They have evolved over the 4.6 billion year history of the earth.

It is instructive to reflect on the way in which earth–based biological evolution spent its time. Single cell entities arose out of the primordial soup roughly 3.5 billion years ago. A billion years passed before photosynthetic plants appeared. After almost another billion and a half years, around 550 million years ago, the first fish and vertebrates arrived, and then insects 450 million years ago. Then things started moving fast. Reptiles arrived 370 million years ago, followed by dinosaurs at 330 and mammals at 250 million years ago. The first primates appeared 120 million years ago and the immediate predecessors to the great apes a mere 18 million years ago. Man arrived in roughly his present form 2.5 million years ago. He invented agriculture a mere 19000 years ago, writing less than 5000 years ago and "expert" knowledge only over the last few hundred years.

This suggests that problem solving behavior, language, expert knowledge and application, and reason, are all rather simple once the essence of being and reacting are available. That essence is the ability to move around in a dynamic environment, sensing the surroundings to a degree sufficient to achieve the necessary maintenance of life and reproduction.

This part of intelligence is where evolution has concentrated its time—it is much harder. This is the physically grounded part of animal systems.

An alternative argument to the preceeding is that in fact once evolution had symbols and representations things started moving rather quickly. Thus symbols are the key invention and AI workers can sidestep the early morass and start working directly with symbols. But I think this misses a critical point, as is shown by the relatively weaker performance of symbol based mobile robots as opposed to physically grounded robots. Without a carefully built physical grounding any symbolic representation will be mismatched to its sensors and actuators. These groundings provide the constraints on symbols necessary for them to be truly useful.

Moravec (1984b) has argued rather eloquently that mobility, acute vision and the ability to carry out survival related tasks in a dynamic environment provide a necessary basis for the development of true intelligence.

3.2   The Subsumption Architecture

In order to explore the construction of physically grounded systems we have developed a computational architecture known as the *subsumption architecture*. It enables us to tightly connect perception to action, embedding robots concretely in the world.

A subsumption program is built on a computational substrate that is organized into a series of incremental layers, each, in the general case, connecting perception to action. In our case the substrate is networks of finite state machines augmented with timing elements.

The subsumption architecture was described initially in Brooks (1986) and later modified in Brooks (1989) and Connell (1989). The subsumption compiler compiles augmented finite state machine (AFSM) descriptions into a special-purpose scheduler to simulate parallelism and a set of finite state machine simulation routines. This is a dynamically retargetable compiler that has backends for a number of processors, including the Motorola 68000, the Motorola 68HC11, and the Hitachi 6301. The subsumption compiler takes a source file as input and produces an assembly language program as output.

The behavior language was inspired by Maes (1989) as a way of grouping AFSMs into more manageable units with the capability for whole units being selectively activated or de-activated. In fact, AFSMs are not specified directly, but rather as rule sets of real-time rules which compile into AFSMs in a one-to-one manner. The behavior compiler is machine-independent and compiles into an intermediate file of subsumption AFSM specifications. The subsumption compiler can then be used to compile to the various targets. We sometimes call the behavior language the *new subsumption*.

The old subsumption language

Each augmented finite state machine (AFSM) has a set of registers and a set of timers, or alarm clocks, connected to a conventional finite state machine which can control a combinational network fed by the registers. Registers can be written by attaching input wires to them and sending messages from other machines. The messages get written into the registers by replacing any existing contents. The arrival of a message, or the expiration of a timer, can trigger a change of state in the interior finite state machine. Finite state machine states can either wait on some event, conditionally dispatch to one of two other states based on some combinational predicate on the registers, or compute a combinational function of the registers directing the result either back to one of the registers or to an output of the augmented finite state machine. Some AFSMs connect directly to robot hardware. Sensors deposit their values in certain registers, and certain outputs direct commands to actuators.

A series of layers of such machines can be augmented by adding new machines and connecting them into the existing network in a number of ways. New inputs can be connected to existing registers, which might previously have contained a constant. New machines can inhibit existing outputs or suppress existing inputs, by being attached as side-taps to existing wires. When a message arrives on an inhibitory side-tap no messages can travel along the existing wire for some short time period. To maintain inhibition there must be a continuous flow of messages along the new wire. (In previous versions of the subsumption architecture (Brooks 1986) explicit, long time periods had to be specified for inhibition or suppression with single shot messages. Recent work has suggested this better approach (Connell 1989).) When a message arrives on a suppressing side-tap, again no messages are allowed to flow from the original source for some small time period, but now the suppressing message is gated through and it masquerades as having come from the original source. A continuous supply of suppressing messages is required to maintain control of a side-tapped wire.

Inhibition and suppression are the mechanisms by which conflict resolution between actuator commands from different layers is achieved. Notice that in this definition of the subsumption architecture, AFSMs cannot share any state, and in particular they each completely encapsulate their own registers and alarm clocks.

All clocks in a subsumption system have approximately the same tick period (0.04 seconds in most of our robots). However, neither the

clocks nor the messages are synchronous. The fastest possible rate of
sending messages along a wire is one per clock tick. The time periods
used for both inhibition and suppression are two clock ticks. Thus, a
side-tapping wire with messages being sent at the maximum rate can
maintain control of its host wire. We call this rate the *characteristic
frequency* of the particular subsumption implementation.

The new subsumption language

The behavior language groups multiple processes (each of which usually
turns out to be implemented as a single AFSM) into *behaviors*. There
can be message passing, suppression, and inhibition between processes
within a behavior, and there can be message passing, suppression and
inhibition between behaviors. Behaviors act as abstraction barriers; one
behavior cannot reach inside another.

Each process within a behavior is much like an AFSM and indeed our
compiler for the behavior language converts them to AFSMs. However,
they are generalized so that they can share registers. A new structure,
monostables, provides a slightly more general timing mechanism than
the original alarm clocks. Monostables are retriggerable, and can be
shared between processes within a single behavior.

4   Some Physically Grounded Systems

In this section we briefly review some previous successful robots built
with the subsumption architecture and highlight the ways in which they
have exploited or epitomize that architecture. The family portrait of all
the robots is shown in Figure 1. Most of the robots were programmed
with the old subsumption language. Toto and Seymour use the new
behavior language.

A key thing to note with these robots is the ways in which seemingly
goal-directed behavior emerges from the interactions of simpler non goal-
directed behaviors.

4.1   Allen

Our first robot, Allen, had sonar range sensors and odometry onboard
and used an offboard lisp machine to simulate the subsumption architecture. In Brooks (1986) we described three layers of control implemented
in the subsumption architecture.

The first layer let the robot avoid both static and dynamic obstacles;
Allen would happily sit in the middle of a room until approached, then
scurry away, avoiding collisions as it went. The internal representation

Figure 1: The MIT Mobile Robots include, in the back row, left to right; Allen, Herbert, Seymour, and Toto. In front row are Tito, Genghis, Squirt (very small), Tom and Jerry, and Labnav.

used was that every sonar return represented a repulsive force with an inverse square decrease in strength as a function of distance. The vector sum of the repulsive forces, suitably thresholded, told the robot in which direction it should move. An additional reflex halted the robot whenever there was something right in front of the robot and it was moving forward (rather than turning in place).

The second layer made the robot randomly wander about. Every 10 seconds or so, a desire to head in a random direction would be generated. That desire was coupled with the reflex to avoid obstacles by vector addition. The summed vector suppressed the more primitive obstacle avoidance vector, but the obstacle avoidance behavior still operated, having been subsumed by the new layer, in its account of the lower level's repulsive force. Additionally, the halt reflex of the lower level operated autonomously and unchanged.

The third layer made the robot look (with its sonars) for distant places and try to head towards them. This layer monitored progress through odometry, generating a desired heading which suppressed the direction desired by the wander layer. The desired heading was then fed into a vector addition with the instinctive obstacle avoidance layer. The physical robot did not therefore remain true to the desires of the upper layer. The upper layer had to watch what happened in the world, through odometry, in order to understand what was really happening in the lower control layers, and send down correction signals.

In Brooks & Connell (1986) we described an alternate set of layers for the robot Allen.

4.2   Tom and Jerry

Tom and Jerry (Connell 1987) were two identical robots built to demonstrate just how little raw computation is necessary to support the subsumption architecture. A three layer subsumption program was implemented, yet all data paths were just one bit wide and the whole program fitted on a single 256 gate programmable array logic chip. Physically Tom and Jerry were toy cars with three one-bit infrared proximity sensors mounted on the front and one at the rear. The sensors were individually tuned to a specific distance at which they would fire. The central front sensor fired only on much closer objects than the two side sensors, which pointed slightly outward.

The lowest layer of Tom and Jerry implemented the standard pair of first level behaviors. These used a vector sum of repulsive forces from obstacles to perform an avoidance manuever or to trigger a halt reflex to stop when something was too close ahead, as detected by the central front looking sensor. There were extra complications with Tom and Jerry in that we needed to use the subsumption architecture to implement an active braking scheme because of the high speed of the robots relative to their sensor ranges. Tom and Jerry's second layers were much like Allen's original second layer—an urge to wander about, which was implemented by an attractive force which got added to the repulsive forces from obstacles. The third layer detected moving objects using the front three sensors and created a following behavior. When something was detected, the robot was attracted and moved towards it. The lower level collide behavior stopped the robot from actually hitting the target, however. While the robot was chasing its target, the wander behavior was suppressed.

Tom and Jerry demonstrated the notion of independent behaviors combining without knowing about each other (chasing obstacles but staying back from them a little). Tom and Jerry also demonstrated that the subsumption architecture could be compiled (by hand) down to the gate level, and that it could be run at clock speeds of only a few hundred Hertz.

4.3   Herbert

Herbert (Brooks, Connell & Ning 1988) was a much more ambitious robot. It has a 24-processor distributed, loosely coupled, onboard computer to run the subsumption architecture. The processors were slow CMOS 8-bit microprocessors (which ran on low electrical power; an important consideration when carrying batteries), which could communicate only by slow serial interfaces (maximum 10 packets each, 24 bits wide per second). Onboard Herbert, the interconnections between AFSMs are physically embodied as actual copper wires.

Herbert had 30 infrared proximity sensors for local obstacle avoidance, an onboard manipulator with a number of simple sensors attached to the hand, and a laser light striping system to collect three dimensional depth data in a 60 degree wide swath in front of the robot with a range of about 12 feet. A 256 pixel-wide by 32 pixel-high depth image was collected every second. Through a special purpose distributed serpentine memory, four of the onboard 8-bit processors were each able to expend about 30 instructions on each data pixel. By linking the processors in a chain we were able to implement quite high performance vision algorithms.

Connell (1989) programmed Herbert to wander around office areas, go into people's offices and steal empty soda cans from their desks. He demonstrated obstacle avoidance and wall following, real-time recognition of soda-can-like objects, and a set of 15 behaviors (Connell 1988) which drove the arm to physically search for a soda can in front of the robot, locate it, and pick it up.

Herbert showed many instances of using the world as its own best model and as a communication medium. The remarkable thing about Herbert is that there was absolutely no internal communication between any of its behavior generating modules. Each one was connected to sensors on the input side, and an arbitration network on the output side. The arbitration network drove the actuators.

The laser-based soda-can object finder drove the robot so that its arm was lined up in front of the soda can. But it did not tell the arm controller that there was now a soda can ready to be picked up. Rather, the arm behaviors monitored the shaft encoders on the wheels, and when they noticed that there was no body motion, initiated motions of the arm, which in turn triggered other behaviors, so that eventually the robot would pick up the soda can.

The advantage of this approach is that there is no need to set up internal expectations for what is going to happen next; this means that the control system can both (1) be naturally opportunistic if fortuitous circumstances present themselves, and (2) it can easily respond to changed circumstances, such as some other object approaching it on a collision course.

As one example of how the arm behaviors cascaded upon one another, consider actually grasping a soda can. The hand had a grasp reflex that operated whenever something broke an infrared beam between the fingers. When the arm located a soda can with its local sensors, it simply drove the hand so that the two fingers lined up on either side of the can. The hand then independently grasped the can. Given this arrangement, it was possible for a human to hand a soda can to the robot. As soon as it was grasped, the arm retracted—it did not matter whether it was a soda can that was intentionally grasped, or one that magically appeared. The same opportunism among behaviors let the arm adapt automatically to a wide variety of cluttered desktops, and still successfully find the soda can.

4.4   Genghis

Genghis (Brooks 1989) is a 1Kg six legged robot which walks under subsumption control and has an extremely distributed control system. The robot successfully walks over rough terrain using 12 motors, 12 force sensors, 6 pyroelectric sensors, one inclinometer and 2 whiskers. It also follows cooperative humans using its pyroelectric sensors.

The subsumption layers successively enable the robot to stand up, walk without any sensing, use force measurements to comply with rough terrain, use force measurements to lift its legs over obstacles, use inclinometer measurements to selectively inhibit rough terrain compliance when appropriate, use whiskers to lift feet over obstacles, use passive infrared sensors to detect people and to walk only when they are present, and to use the directionality of infrared radiation to modulate the backswing of leg sets so that the robot follows a moving source of radiation.

In contrast, one could imagine a control system which had a central repository which modeled the robot's configuration in translation and orientation space. One could further imagine high level commands (for instance from a path planner) generating updates for the robot's coordinates. These high level commands would then be hierarchically resolved into instructions for individual legs.

The control system on Genghis has no such repository. Indeed there is not even a central repository for each leg—separate motors on the legs are controlled quite separately in different parts of the network. While there is a some semblance of a central control system for each individual motor, these controllers receive messages from diverse parts of the network and simply pass them on to the motors, without any attempt at integration.

Our control system was also very easy to build. It was built incrementally, with each new capability being a simple of addition (no deletion, no change to previous network) of new network structure. The debugged existing network structure was never altered.

The resulting control system is elegant in its simplicity. It does not deal with coordinate transforms or kinematic models. It is not at all hierarchical. It directly implements walking through many very tight couplings of sensors to actuators. It is very distributed in its nature, and we believe its robustness in handling rough terrain comes from this distributed form of control.

We are currently building a new version of Genghis (Angle 1989a) which will be a much stronger climber and able to scramble at around three kilometers per hour. Each leg has three degrees of freedom and three force sensors mounted on load bearing beams. A single-chip microprocessor with onboard RAM and EEPROM is easily able to force servo the complete leg. The total mass of the final robot will 1.6 Kg. Attila will have batteries which will power it for about 30 minutes while actively walking. Following that, it will have to recharge from solar cells for about 4.5 hours in Earth sunlight.

4.5 Squirt

Squirt is the smallest robot we have built (Flynn, Brooks, Wells & Barrett 1989b). It weighs about 50 grams and is about 5/4 cubic inches in volume.

Squirt incorporates an 8-bit computer, an onboard power supply, three sensors and a propulsion system. Its normal mode of operation is to act as a "bug", hiding in dark corners and venturing out in the direction of noises, only after the noises are long gone, looking for a new place to hide near where the previous set of noises came from.

The most interesting thing about Squirt is the way in which this high level behavior emerges from a set of simple interactions with the world.

Squirt's lowest level of behavior monitors a light sensor and causes it to move in a spiral pattern searching for darkness. The spiral trajectories are created by a coupling of a forward motion along with a back-and-turn motion, implemented through the use of only one motor and made possible by a unidirectional clutch on the rear axle. Once Squirt finds a dark spot, it stops.

Squirt's second level of behavior is triggered once a dark hiding place has been established. This behavior monitors two microphones and measures the time of arrival of sound at each microphone. By noting the difference, it can localize the direction from which the sound came. Squirt then waits for a pattern of a sharp noise followed by a few minutes of silence. If this pattern is recognized, Squirt ventures out in the direction of the last heard noise, suppressing the desire to stay in the dark. After this ballistic straight-line motion times out, the lower level is no longer suppressed and the light sensor is again recognized. If it is light, the spiraling pattern kicks back in. The end effect is that Squirt gravitates towards the center of action. The entire compiled control system for Squirt fits in 1300 bytes of code on an onboard microprocessor.

4.6   Toto

Toto (Mataric 1989) is our first robot fully programmed with the new behavior language. Toto has 12 radially arranged sonars and a flux-gate compass as its sensors.

At first appearances it may seem that the subsumption architecture does not allow for such conventional items as maps. There are no data structures within the subsumption architecture, and no easy way of having a central repository for more than simple numeric quantities. Our work with Toto demonstrates that these are not critical limitations with regard to map building and use.

Toto has a low level reactive system to keep basic functions running robustly. Its lower level behaviors enable it to wander around avoiding collisions, and successfully follow walls and corridors as if it were explicitly exploring the world. An intermediate level set of behaviors tries to recognize particular types of landmark such as walls, corridors and clutter. Another network is made up of mutually identical behaviors wtih each layer waiting for new landmarks to be recognized. Each time this happens a behavior allocates itself to be the 'place' of that particular landmark. The behaviors which correspond to physically adjacent landmarks have neighbor relationship links activated between them. A graph structure is thus formed, although the nodes are active computational elements rather than static data structures. (In fact, each node is really a whole collection of compuational elements in the form of augmented finite state machines.)

As the robot moves around the environment, the nodes try to keep track of where it is. Nodes become more active if they believe that they correspond to the place at which the robot is currently located. Thus the robot has both a map, and a sense of where it is on the map, but using a totally distributed computational model.

When a behavior (such as "go to some place") is activated (via a small panel of push buttons on the robot) a spreading of activation mechanism is used, which spreads from the goal via the neighbor links. This process is continuous and keeps the robot informed as it reaches each place expected from the map.

Mataric (1990a)'s experimental results show how the robot's performance can be incrementally improved by adding new pieces of network. Map building and path planning were initially demonstrated with fewer types of behaviors than finally implemented. Then an idea of expectation, based on temporally generated context was added. This allowed the robot to handle getting lost and and to relocate itself in the map later. Then a coarse position estimatation scheme was added, based on integrating the compass heading over time. This significantly lowered the level of ambiguity in both map building and map use in more complex environments, and thus increased the robot's overall competence. In all cases we simply added new behaviors to the netwrok to improve the map building and using performance.

The work has also shown that globally consistent maps can be built and emerge in a totally distributed manner. In our experiments they were built by a collection of asynchronous independent agents, without the abililty to use arbitrary pointers, or other such traditional data structure techniques. In path planning there is no notion of a global path under this scheme; local pieces of information combine to direct the robot through its dynamics of interaction with the world, to get to the desired place. Overall, these aspects demonstrate that the techniques should scale well.

It has been easy to integrate the maps with the dynamics of navigation, obstacle avoidance and path planning. The representations have a natural ability to integrate temporal aspects of the dynamics since they can use time as its own representation!

The notion of place maps developed for Toto bears striking similarities to what has been observed in the hippocampus of the rat (Eichenbaum, Wiener, Shapiro & Cohen 1989).

4.7   Seymour

Seymour is a new robot we are building with all onboard processing to support vision processing of 9 low resolution cameras at approximately 10 frames per second (Brooks & Flynn 1989). The cameras feed into different subsumption layers which act upon those aspects of the world they perceive. Seymour is also programmed in the new behavior language.

A number of vision based behaviors developed for Seymour have been prototyped on earlier robots.

Horswill & Brooks (1988) describe a subsumption program that controls two simple and unreliable visual processing routines to produce a reliable behavior which follows moving objects using vision. One vision process tracks a single moving blob. It gets bootstrapped by another process which overlays the blob image with an indication of where motion is seen. The robot then tries to servo a selected blob to stay in a fixed location in image coordinates. The blob tracker often loses the blob it is tracking. The motion finder produces a lot of noise especially when the robot is moving, but between the two of them they let the robot reliably follow a moving object (any moving object; we have seen the robot chase a black trash can dragged by a string, a radio controlled toy blue car on a blue floor, a pink plastic flamingo, a grey notebook on a grey carpeted floor, and a drinking mug moved around by hand), by switching back and forth between the visual routines as either one fails. Nowhere internally does the subsumption program have the notion of an identifiable object, yet to an outside observer it certainly appears to follow a moving object very well.

Using the robot Tito, Sarachik (1989) demonstrated two visually guided behaviors which will be used in support of Seymour. Each behavior used a stereo pair of linear cameras. A vertically mounted pair made use of rotational motions of the base to produce images from which the dimensions of the room could be extracted even though the camera system was uncalibrated. Then employing earlier results from Brooks, Flynn & Marill (1987), the robot motion to calibrate a horizontally mounted pair of cameras, which were used to find doorways through which the robot drove.

Viola (1989) has demonstrated an autonomous eyeball capable of maintaining a steady gaze despite motion of its platform. It recapitulates the primate vestibular-occular system by using vision as a slow calibration system for a gyroscope controlled movable platform which holds the camera.

4.8   Gnat Robots

In all our use and development of the subsumption architecture we have been careful to maitain its simplicitly so that programs written in it could be easily and mechanically compiled into silicon. For example with Toto the map networks were arranged so that the total wire length for connecting the underlying finite state machines need be no more than linear in the number of finite state machines. In general the area of silicon needed for the robots we have built would be quite small. There is a reason for maintaining this restriction.

Flynn (1989) and Flynn (1988) introduced the idea of building complete small robots out of silicon on a VLSI fabrication line. Brooks (1987) demonstrated how to use the subsumption architecture to control such robots. There is great potential for using such robots in ways previously not considered at all cost effective for robotic applications. Imagine for instance having a colony of tiny robots living on your TV screen, absorbing energy from the electron beam, whose only purpose in existence is to keep the screen clean. There is potential for a revolution in micro-mechanical systems of the same order and impact as the quiet revolutions brought about in daily life by the advent of the micro-processor.

Flynn et al. (1989a) outlines a series of technological steps necessary to build such robots, including materials, a new type of micro motor based on thin film piezo-electric material, a 3-D fabrication process, and some new types of integrated sensors. Critical to this enterprise is an easy way of controlling the robots, giving them intelligent behavior in unstructured and uncertain environments.

5   Measures of Success

When I give talks about the techniques we have used to build intelligent control systems for our robots, the most common questions I am asked, or assertions I am told, are:

- "If a make *such-and-such* a change to your robot's environment, I bet it would do the wrong thing."

- "Aren't these systems almost impossible to debug?"

- "Surely this can't be scaled up to do X", for some value of X which has not been part of the talk.

In the next three subsections I argue that these questions are either easy to answer or, in a deep sense, improper to ask.

5.1   Puzzlitis

Since traditional Artificial Intelligence research has concentrated on isolated modules of intelligence that almost never get grounded in the world, it has been important to develop some criteria for successful research. One of the most popular ideas is generality. This quickly leads to a disease I call *puzzlitis*. The way to show generality is to pick the most obscure case within the domain and demonstrate that your system can handle or solve it.

But in physically grounded systems I believe this approach is counterproductive. The puzzles posed are often very unlikely in practice, but to solve them makes the systems much more complex. This reduces the overall robustness of the system! We should be driven by puzzles which can naturally arise in a physically grounded context—this is what gives strength to our physically grounded systems.

One additional argument on this topic is that for most AI programs the creator gets to tell the program the facts in some sort of representation language. It is assumed that the vision guys in the white hats down the corridor will one day deliver world models using these same representations. Many of the puzzlitis failures of physically grounded systems stem from a failure in perception as the stakes have been raised. Standard AI programs have not been forced to face these issues.

5.2 Debugging

In our experience debugging the subsumption programs used to control our physically grounded systems has not been a great source of frustration or difficulty. This is not due to any particularly helpful debugging tools or any natural superiority of the subsumption architecture.

Rather, we believe it is true because the world is its own best model (as usual). When running a physically grounded system in the real world, one can see at a glance how it is interacting. It is right before your eyes. There are no layers of abstraction to obfuscate the dynamics of the interactions between the system and the world. This is an elegant aspect of physically grounded systems.

5.3 But It Can't Do X

Along with the statement "But it can't do X" there is an implication, sometimes vocalized, and sometimes not, that therefore there are lots of things that this approach is not good for, and so we should resort to the symbol system hypothesis.

But this is a fallacious argument, even if only implicit. We do not usually complain that a medical expert system, or an analogy program cannot climb real mountains. It is clear that their domain of expertise is somewhat more limited, and that their designers were careful to pick a well circumscribed domain in which to work. Likewise it is unfair to claim that an elephant has no intelligence worth studying just because it does not play chess.

People working on physically grounded systems do, however, seem to be claiming to eventually solve the whole problem. E.g., papers such as this one, argue that this in an interesting approach to pursue for precisely that reason. How can we have it both ways?

Like the advocates of the symbol system hypothesis, we believe that in principle we have uncovered the fundamental foundation of intelligence. But just as the symbol system people are allowed to work incrementally in their goals, so should the physical grounding people.

Solutions to all problems are not obvious now. We must spend time, analyzing the needs of certain domains *from the perspective of the physical grounding hypothesis* to discern what new structures and abstractions must be built in order to make forward progress.

6   Future Limits

As Simon (1969) points out, concerning his symbol system hypothesis:

> The hypothesis is clearly an empirical one, to be judged true or false on the basis of evidence.

The same can, of course, be said for the physical grounding hypothesis.

Our current strategy is to test the limitations of the physical grounding hypothesis by building robots which are more independent and can do more in the world. We are tackling aspects of human competence in a different order than that chosen by people working under the symbol system hypothesis, so sometimes it is hard to make comparisons between the relative successes. A further part of our strategy then, is to build systems that can be deployed in the real world. At least if our strategy does not convince the arm chair philosophers, our engineering approach will have radically changed the world we live in.

6.1   Contrasts In Hope

Adherents of both approaches to intelligence are relying on some degree of hope that their approach will eventually succeed. They have both demonstrated certain classes of success, but both can resort only to vague hopes when it comes to generalizability. It turns out that the demonstrations and generalization issues fall along different dimensions for the two approaches.

- Traditional AI has tried to demonstrate sophisticated reasoning in rather impoverished domains. The hope is that the ideas used will generalize to robust behavior in more complex domains.

- Nouvelle AI tries to demonstrate less sophisticated tasks operating robustly in noisy complex domains. The hope is that the ideas used will generalize to more sophisticated tasks.

Thus the two approaches appear somewhat complementary. It is worth addressing the question of whether more power may be gotten by combining the two approaches. However, we will not pursue that question further here.

Both approaches rely on some unanalyzed aspects to gain their successes.

Traditional AI relies on the use of heuristics to control search. While much mathematical analysis has been carried out on this topic, the user of a heuristic still relies on an expected distribution of cases within the search tree to get a "reasonable" amount of pruning in order to make the problem manageable.

Nouvelle AI relies on the emergence of more global behavior from the interaction of smaller behavioral units. As with heuristics there is no a priori guarantee that this will always work. However, careful design of the simple behaviors and their interactions can often produce systems with useful and interesting emergent properties. The user again is relying on expectations without hard proofs.

Can there be a theoretical analysis to decide whether one organization for intelligence is better than another? Perhaps, but I think we are so far away from understanding the correct way of formalizing the dynamics of interaction with the environment, that no such theoretical results will be forthcoming in the near term.

6.2   Specific Problems

Some of the specific problems which must be tackled soon, and solved, by approaches to AI based on the physical grounding hypothesis include

- how to combine many (e.g. more than a dozen) behavior generating modules in a way which lets them be productive and cooperative

- how to handle multiple sources of perceptual information when there really does seem to be a need for fusion

- how to automate the building of interaction interfaces between behavior generating modules, so that larger (and hence more competent) systems can be built

- how to automate the construction of individual behavior generating modules, or even to automate their modification

The first two items have specific impact on whether the approach can scale in principle to larger and more complex tasks. The last two are concerned with the issue of how to build such larger systems even if they are in principle possible.

There is room for plenty of experimentation, and eventually, when we are mature enough, there is also room for much theoretical development of the approaches to Artificial Intelligence based on the physical grounding hypothesis.

Acknowledgements

Pattie Maes encouraged me to write this paper, despite my earlier refusal to do so. She and Maja Mataric made a number of useful criticisms of an earlier draft of this paper.

Funding for this work was provided by a number of government agencies and companies including: the University Research Initiative under Office of Naval Research contract N00014–86–K–0685, the Defense Advanced Research Projects Agency under Office of Naval Research contract N00014–85–K–0124, Hughes Research Laboratories Artificial Intelligence Center in Malibu, Siemens Research Center in Princeton, and Mazda Research Center in Yokohama.

CHAPTER 8
· ·
INTELLIGENCE WITHOUT REASON

In 1991 I was co-winner of the Computers and Thought *prize at the International Joint Conference on Artificial Intelligence (IJCAI), awarded every two years for outstanding research to a young AI researcher. Apart from forcing the organization to reconsider what* young *meant given my now advancing age (and under the new rules I would not have been eligible in 1991), this was the greatest honor that the AI community could bestow upon me, and I was quite touched that they should put aside their arguments with me to do so. They invited me to contribute a paper to the proceedings and waived the six page length limit—this was a mistake on their part as can be seen from the length of this paper, my contribution. I took the opportunity to deconstruct how classical Artificial Intelligence had come to be in the state that it was in, and in particular how the structure of* computers *and self-introspection about* thought *had influenced its directions. I also took the opportunity to use my bully-pulpit to outline how the behavior-based approaches were much more like real biological systems than was classical Artificial Intelligence. Today there are large parts of Artificial Intelligence that have moved in similar directions and there are many specialized conferences where the newer themes outlined below are the ones that dominate. But IJCAI itself continues in its old ways; hardly a whiff of the new approaches can be smelled in its crusty sessions.*

Abstract. *Computers* and *Thought* are the two categories that together define Artificial Intelligence as a discipline. It is generally accepted that work in Artificial Intelligence over the last thirty years has had a strong influence on aspects of computer architectures. In this paper we also make the converse claim; that the state of computer architecture has been a strong influence on our models of thought. The

Originally appeared in the *Proceedings of the 1991 International Joint Conference on Artificial Intelligence*, 1991, pp. 569–595.

Von Neumann model of computation has lead Artificial Intelligence in particular directions. Intelligence in biological systems is completely different. Recent work in behavior-based Artificial Intelligence has produced new models of intelligence that are much closer in spirit to biological systems. The non-Von Neumann computational models they use share many characteristics with biological computation.

1   Introduction

Artificial Intelligence as a formal discipline has been around for a little over thirty years. The goals of individual practitioners vary and change over time. A reasonable characterization of the general field is that it is intended to make computers do things, that when done by people, are described as having indicated intelligence. Winston (1984) characterizes the goals of Artificial Intelligence as both the construction of useful intelligent systems and the understanding of human intelligence.

There is a temptation (often succumbed to) to then go ahead and define *intelligence*, but that does not immediately give a clearly grounded meaning to the field. In fact there is danger of deep philosophical regress with no recovery. Therefore I prefer to stay with a more informal notion of intelligence being the sort of stuff that humans do, pretty much all the time.

1.1   Approaches

Traditional Artificial Intelligence has tried to tackle the problem of building artificially intelligent systems from the top down. It tackled intelligence through the notions of *thought* and *reason*. These are things we only know about through introspection. The field has adopted a certain *modus operandi* over the years, which includes a particular set of conventions on how the inputs and outputs to thought and reasoning are to be handled (e.g., the subfield of knowledge representation), and the sorts of things that thought and reasoning do (e.g., planning, problem solving, etc.). I will argue that these conventions cannot account for large aspects of what goes into intelligence. Furthermore, without those aspects the validity of the traditional Artificial Intelligence approaches comes into question. I will also argue that much of the landmark work on thought has been influenced by the technological constraints of the available computers, and thereafter these consequences have often mistakenly become enshrined as principles, long after the original impetus has disappeared.

From an evolutionary stance, human level intelligence did not suddenly leap onto the scene. There were precursors and foundations throughout the lineage to humans. Much of this substrate is present in other animals today. The study of that substrate may well provide constraints on how higher level *thought* in humans could be organized.

Recently there has been a movement to study intelligence from the bottom up, concentrating on physical systems (e.g., mobile robots), situated in the world, autonomously carrying out tasks of various sorts. Some of this work is based on engineering from first principles, other parts of the work are firmly based on biological inspirations. The flavor of this work is quite different from that of traditional Artificial Intelligence. In fact it suggests that despite our best introspections, traditional Artificial Intelligence offers solutions to intelligence which bear almost no resemblance at all to how biological systems work.

There are of course dangers in studying biological systems too closely. Their design was not highly optimized from a global systems point of view. Rather they were patched together and adapted from previously working systems, in ways which most expeditiously met the latest environmental pressures. Perhaps the solutions found for much of intelligence are terribly suboptimal. Certainly there are many vestigial structures surviving within humans' and other animals' digestive, skeletal, and muscular systems. One should suppose then that there are many vestigial neurological structures, interactions, and side effects. Their emulation may be a distraction.

1.2   Outline

The body of this paper is formed by five main sections: 2 *Robots*, 3 *Computers*, 4 *Biology*, 5 *Ideas* and 6 *Thought*. The theme of the paper is how computers and thought have be intimately intertwined in the development of Artificial Intelligence, how those connections may have led the field astray, how biological examples of intelligence are quite different from the models used by Artificial Intelligence, and how recent new approaches point to another path for both computers and thought.

The new approaches that have been developed recently for Artificial Intelligence arose out of work with mobile robots. Section 2 (Robots) briefly outlines the context within which this work arose, and discusses some key realizations made by the researchers involved.

Section 3 (Computers) traces the development of the foundational ideas for Artificial Intelligence, and how they were intimately linked to the technology available for computation. Neither situatedness nor embodiment were easy to include on the original agenda, although their importance was recognized by many early researchers. The early framework with its emphasis on search has remained dominant, and has led to solutions that seem important within the closed world of Artificial

Intelligence, but which perhaps are not very relevant to practical applications. The field of Cybernetics with a heritage of very different tools from the early digital computer, provides an interesting counterpoint, confirming the hypothesis that models of thought are intimately tied to the available models of computation.

Section 4 (Biology) is a brief overview of recent developments in the understanding of biological intelligence. It covers material from ethology, psychology, and neuroscience. Of necessity it is not comprehensive, but it is sufficient to demonstrate that the intelligence of biological systems is organized in ways quite different from traditional views of Artificial Intelligence.

Section 5 (Ideas) introduces the two cornerstones to the new approach to Artificial Intelligence, *situatedness* and *embodiment*, and discusses both intelligence and emergence in these contexts.

The last major section, 6 (Thought), outlines some details of the approach of my group at MIT to building complete situated, embodied, artificially intelligent robots. This approach shares much more heritage with biological systems than with what is usually called Artificial Intelligence.

2   Robots

There has been a scattering of work with mobile robots within the Artificial Intelligence community over the years. Shakey from the late sixties at SRI (see Nilsson (1984) for a collection of original reports) is perhaps the best known, but other significant efforts include the CART (Moravec 1983) at Stanford and Hilare (Giralt et al. 1984) in Toulouse.

All these systems used offboard computers (and thus they could be the largest most powerful computers available at the time and place), and all operated in mostly[1] static environments. All of these robots operated in environments that at least to some degree had been specially engineered for them. They all sensed the world and tried to build two or three dimensional world models of it. Then, in each case, a planner could ignore the actual world, and operate in the model to produce a plan of action for the robot to achieve whatever goal it had been given. In all

---

[1] In the case of Shakey, experiments included the existence of a gremlin who would secretly come and alter the environment by moving a block to a different location. However, this would usually happen only once, say, in a many hour run, and the robot would not perceive the dynamic act, but rather might later notice a changed world if the change was directly relevant to the particular subtask it was executing. In the case of the CART, the only dynamic aspect of the world was the change in sun angle over long time periods, and this in fact caused the robot to fail as its position estimation scheme was confused by the moving shadows.

three of these robots, the generated plans included at least a nominal path through the world model along which it was intended that the robot should move.

Despite the simplifications (static, engineered environments, and the most powerful available computers) all these robots operated excruciatingly slowly. Much of the processing time was consumed in the perceptual end of the systems and in building the world models. Relatively little computation was used in planning and acting.

An important effect of this work was to provide a framework within which other researchers could operate without testing their ideas on real robots, and even without having any access to real robot data. We will call this framework, the *sense-model-plan-act* framework, or *SMPA* for short. See section 3.6 for more details of how the SMPA framework influenced the manner in which robots were built over the following years, and how those robots in turn imposed restrictions on the ways in which intelligent control programs could be built for them.

There was at least an implicit assumption in this early work with mobile robots, that once the simpler case of operating in a static environment had been solved, then the more difficult case of an actively dynamic environment could be tackled. None of these early SMPA systems were ever extended in this way.

Around 1984, a number of people started to worry about the more general problem of organizing intelligence. There was a requirement that intelligence be reactive to dynamic aspects of the environment, that a mobile robot operate on time scales similar to those of animals and humans, and that intelligence be able to generate robust behavior in the face of uncertain sensors, an unpredicted environment, and a changing world. Some of the key realizations about the organization of intelligence were as follows:

- Most of what people do in their day to day lives is not problem-solving or planning, but rather it is routine activity in a relatively benign, but certainly dynamic, world. Furthermore the representations an agent uses of objects in the world need not rely on a semantic correspondence with symbols that the agent possesses, but rather can be defined through interactions of the agent with the world. Agents based on these ideas have achieved interesting performance levels and were built from combinatorial circuits plus a little timing circuitry (Agre & Chapman 1987), (Agre & Chapman 1990).

- An observer can legitimately talk about an agent's beliefs and goals, even though the agent need not manipulate symbolic data structures at run time. A formal grounding in semantics used for the agent's design can be compiled away. Agents based on these ideas have achieved interesting performance levels and were built from combinatorial circuits plus a little timing circuitry (Rosenschein & Kaelbling 1986*b*), (Kaelbling & Rosenschein 1990).

- In order to really test ideas of intelligence it is important to build complete agents which operate in dynamic environments using real sensors. Internal world models which are complete representations of the external environment, besides being impossible to obtain, are not at all necessary for agents to act in a competent manner. Many of the actions of an agent are quite separable— coherent intelligence can emerge from subcomponents interacting in the world. Agents based on these ideas have achieved interesting performance levels and were built from combinatorial circuits plus a little timing circuitry (Brooks 1986), (Brooks 1990*c*), (Brooks 1991*c*).

A large number of others have also contributed to this approach to organizing intelligence. Maes (1990*b*) is the most representative collection.

There is no generally accepted term to describe this style of work. It has sometimes been characterized by the oxymoron *reactive planning.* I have variously used *Robot Beings* (Brooks & Flynn 1989) and *Artificial Creatures* (Brooks 1990*c*). Related work on non-mobile, but nevertheless active, systems has been called *active vision,* or *animate vision* (Ballard 1989). Some workers refer to their beings, or creatures, as *agents*; unfortunately that term is also used by others to refer to somewhat independent components of intelligence within a single physical creature (e.g., the agencies of Minsky (1986)). Sometimes the approach is called *behavior-based* as the computational components tend to be direct behavior producing modules.[2] For the remainder of this paper, we will simply call the entities of discussion 'robots' or 'behavior-based robots'.

There are a number of key aspects characterizing this style of work.

Situatedness: The robots are situated in the world—they do not deal with abstract descriptions, but with the here and now of the world directly influencing the behavior of the system.

Embodiment: The robots have bodies and experience the world directly—their actions are part of a dynamic with the world and have immediate feedback on their own sensations.

---

[2]Unfortunately this clashes a little with the meaning of *behavior* as used by ethologists as an observed interaction with the world, rather than as something explicitly generated.

Intelligence: They are observed to be intelligent—but the source of intelligence is not limited to just the computational engine. It also comes from the situation in the world, the signal transformations within the sensors, and the physical coupling of the robot with the world.

Emergence: The intelligence of the system emerges from the system's interactions with the world and from sometimes indirect interactions between its components—it is sometimes hard to point to one event or place within the system and say that is why some external action was manifested.

Recently there has been a trend to try to integrate traditional symbolic reasoning, on top of a purely reactive system, both with real robots (e.g., Arkin (1990), Mitchell (1990)) and in simulation (e.g., Firby (1989)). The idea is that the reactive system handles the real-time issues of being embedded in the world, while the deliberative system does the 'hard' stuff traditionally imagined to be handled by an Artificial Intelligence system. I think that these approaches are suffering from the well known 'horizon effect'—they have bought a little better performance in their overall system with the reactive component, but they have simply pushed the limitations of the reasoning system a bit further into the future. I will not be concerned with such systems for the remainder of this paper.

Before examining this work in greater detail, we will turn to the reasons why traditional Artificial Intelligence adopted such a different approach.

3   Computers

In evolution there is a theory (Gould & Eldredge 1977) of punctuated equilibria, where most of the time there is little change within a species, but at intervals a subpopulation branches off with a short burst of greatly accelerated changes. Likewise, I believe that in Artificial Intelligence research over the last forty or so years, there have been long periods of incremental work within established guidelines, and occasionally a shift in orientation and assumptions causing a new subfield to branch off. The older work usually continues, sometimes remaining strong, and sometimes dying off gradually. This description of the field also fits more general models of science, such as Kuhn (1970).

The point of this section is that all those steady-state bodies of work rely, sometimes implicitly, on certain philosophical and *technological* assumptions. The founders of the bodies of work are quite aware of these assumptions, but over time as new people come into the fields, these assumptions get lost, forgotten, or buried, and the work takes on a life of its own for its own sake.

In this section I am particularly concerned with how the architecture of our computers influences our choice of problems on which to work, our models of thought, and our algorithms, and how the problems on which we work, our models of thought, and our algorithm choice puts pressure on the development of architectures of our computers.

Biological systems run on massively parallel, low speed computation, within an essentially fixed topology network with bounded depth. Almost all Artificial Intelligence research, and indeed almost all modern computation, runs on essentially Von Neumann architectures, with a large, inactive memory which can respond at very high speed over an extremely narrow channel, to a very high speed central processing unit which contains very little state. When connections to sensors and actuators are also considered, the gap between biological systems and our artificial systems widens.

Besides putting architectural constraints on our programs, even our mathematical tools are strongly influenced by our computational architectures. Most algorithmic analysis is based on the RAM model of computation (essentially a Von Neumann model, shown to be polynomially equivalent to a Turing machine, e.g., Hartmanis (1971)). Only in recent years have more general models gained prominence, but they have been in the direction of oracles, and other improbable devices for our robot beings.

Are we doomed to work forever within the current architectural constraints?

Over the past few centuries computation technology has progressed from making marks on various surfaces (chiselling, writing, etc.), through a long evolutionary chain of purely mechanical systems, then electromechanical relay based systems, through vacuum tube based devices, followed by an evolutionary chain of silicon-based devices to the current state of the art.

It would be the height of arrogance and foolishness to assume that we are now using the ultimate technology for computation, namely silicon based integrated circuits, just as it would have been foolish (at least in retrospect) to assume in the 16th century that Napier's Bones were the ultimate computing technology (Williams 1983). Indeed the end of the exponential increase in computation speed for uni-processors is in sight, forcing somewhat the large amount of research into parallel approaches to more computation for the dollar, and per second. But there are other more radical possibilities for changes in computation infrastructure.[3] These include computation based on optical switching (Gibbs 1985), (Brady 1990), protein folding, gene expression, non-organic atomic switching.

3.1 Prehistory

During the early 1940's even while the second world war was being waged, and the first electronic computers were being built for cryptanalysis and trajectory calculations, the idea of using computers to carry out intelligent activities was already on people's minds.

Alan Turing, already famous for his work on computability (Turing 1937) had discussions with Donald Michie, as early as 1943, and others less known to the modern Artificial Intelligence world as early as 1941, about using a computer to play chess. He and others developed the idea of minimaxing a tree of moves, and of static evaluation, and carried out elaborate hand simulations against human opponents. Later (during the period from 1945 to 1950 at least) he and Claude Shannon communicated about these ideas.[4] Although there was already an established field of mathematics concerning a theory of games, pioneered by Neumann & Morgenstern (1944), chess had such a large space of legal positions, that even though everything about it is deterministic, the theories were not particularly applicable. Only heuristic and operational programs seemed plausible means of attack.

In a paper titled *Intelligent Machinery*, written in 1948,[5] but not published until long after his death (Turing 1970), Turing outlined a more general view of making computers intelligent. In this rather short insightful paper he foresaw many modern developments and techniques. He argued (somewhat whimsically, to the annoyance of his employers (Hodges 1983)) for at least some fields of intelligence, and his particular example is the learning of languages, that the machine would have to be embodied, and claimed success "seems however to depend rather too much on sense organs and locomotion to be feasible".

Turing argued that it must be possible to build a thinking machine since it was possible to build imitations of "any small part of a man." He made the distinction between producing accurate electrical models of nerves, and replacing them computationally with the available technol-

---

[3] Equally radical changes have occurred in the past, but admittedly they happened well before the current high levels of installed base of silicon-based computers.

[4] Norbert Wiener also outlines the idea of minimax in the final note of the original edition of Wiener (1948). However he restricts the idea to a depth of two or three plays—one assumes for practical reasons, as he does express the general notion for n plays. See section 3.3 for more details on the ways in which cybernetic models of thought were restricted by the computational models at hand.

[5] Different sources cite 1947 and 1948 as the time of writing.

ogy of vacuum tube circuits (this follows directly from his earlier paper Turing (1937)), and the assumption that the nervous system can be modeled as a computational system. For other parts of the body he suggests that "television cameras, microphones, loudspeakers," etc., could be used to model the rest of the system. "This would be a tremendous undertaking of course." Even so, Turing notes that the so constructed machine "would still have no contact with food, sex, sport and many other things of interest to the human being." Turing concludes that the best domains in which to explore the mechanization of thought are various games, and cryptanalysis, "in that they require little contact with the outside world."[6]

Turing thus carefully considered the question of embodiment, and for technical reasons chose to pursue aspects of intelligence which could be viewed, at least in his opinion, as purely symbolic. Minimax search, augmented with the idea of pursuing chains of capture to quiescence, and clever static evaluation functions (the *Turochamp* system of David Champernowne and Alan Turing[7], Shannon (1950)) soon became the dominant approach to the problem. Newell, Shaw & Simon (1958) compared all four known implemented chess playing programs of 1958 (with a total combined experience of six games played), including Turochamp, and they all followed this approach.

The basic approach of minimax with a good static evaluation function has not changed to this day. Programs of this ilk compete well with International Grand Masters. The best of them, *Deep Thought* (Hsu, Anantharaman, Campbell & Nowatzyk 1990), uses special purpose chips for massive search capabilities, along with a skillful evaluation scheme and selective deepening to direct that search better than in previous programs.

Although Turing had conceived of using chess as a vehicle for studying human thought processes, this notion has largely gotten lost along the way (there are of course exceptions, e.g., Wilkins (1979) describes a system which substitutes chess knowledge for search in the middle game—usually there are very few static evaluations, and tree search is mainly to confirm or deny the existence of a mate). Instead the driving force has always been performance, and the most successful program of the day has usually relied on technological advances. Brute force tree search has been the dominant method, itself dominated by the amount of

---

[6] Interestingly, Turing did not completely abstract even a chess playing machine away from embodiment, commenting that "its only organs need be 'eyes' capable of distinguishing the various positions on a specially made board, and means for announcing its own moves".

[7] See *Personal Computing* January 1980, pages 80–81, for a description of this hand simulation of a chess machine.

bruteness available. This in turn has been a product of clever harnessing of the latest technology available. Over the years, the current 'champion' program has capitalized on the available hardware. *MacHack-6* (Greenblatt, Eastlake & Crocker 1967) made use of the largest available fast memory (256K 36 bits words—about a megabyte or so, or $45 by today's standards) and a new comprehensive architecture (the PDP-6) largely influenced by Minsky and McCarthy's requirements for Lisp and symbolic programming. *Chess 4.0* and its descendants (Slate & Atkin 1984) relied on the running on the world's faster available computer. *Belle* (Condon & Thompson 1984) used a smaller central computer, but had a custom move generator, built from LSI circuits. Deep Thought, mentioned above as the most recent champion, relies on custom VLSI circuits to handle its move generation and tree search. It is clear that the success and progress in chess playing programs has been driven by technology enabling large tree searches. Few would argue that today's chess programs/hardware systems are very good models for general human thought processes.

There were some misgivings along the way, however. In an early paper Selfridge (1956) argues that better static evaluation is the key to playing chess, so that look-ahead can be limited to a single move except in situations close to mate (and one assumes he would include situations where there is capture, and perhaps exchanges, involved). But, he claims that humans come to chess with a significant advantage over computers (the thrust of the paper is on learning, and in this instance on learning to play chess) as they have concepts such as 'value,' 'double threat,' the 'centre' etc., already formed. Chess to Selfridge is not a disembodied exercise, but one where successful play is built upon a richness of experience in other, perhaps simpler, situations.

There is an interesting counterpoint to the history of computer chess; the game of Go. The search tree for Go is much much larger than for chess, and a good static evaluation function is much harder to define. Go has never worked out well as a vehicle for research in computer game playing—any reasonable crack at it is much more likely to require techniques much closer to those of human thought—mere computer technology advances are not going to bring the minimax approach close to success in this domain (see Campbell (1983) for a brief overview).

Before leaving Turing entirely there is one other rather significant contribution he made to the field which in a sense he predated. Turing (1950) poses the question "Can machines think?" To tease out an acceptable meaning for this question he presented what has come to be known as the *Turing test*, where a person communicates in English over a teletype with either another person or a computer. The goal is to guess whether it is a person or a computer at the other end. Over time this test has come to be an informal goal of Artificial Intelligence.[8] Notice that it is a totally disembodied view of intelligence, although it is somewhat situated in that the machine has to respond in a timely fashion to its interrogator. Turing suggests that the machine should try to simulate a person by taking extra time and making mistakes with arithmetic problems. This is the version of the Turing test that is bandied around by current day Artificial Intelligence researchers.[9]

Turing advances a number of strawman arguments against the case that a digital computer might one day be able to pass this test, but he does not consider the need that the machine be fully embodied. In principle, of course, he is right. But how a machine might be then programmed is a question. Turing provides an argument that programming the machine by hand would be impractical, so he suggests having it learn. At this point he brings up the need to embody the machine in some way. He rejects giving it limbs, but suspects that eyes would be good, although not entirely necessary. At the end of the paper he proposes two possible paths towards his goal of a "thinking" machine. The unembodied path is to concentrate on programming intellectual activities like chess, while the embodied approach is to equip a digital computer "with the best sense organs that money can buy, and then teach it to understand and speak English". Artificial Intelligence followed the former path, and has all but ignored the latter approach.[10]

3.2   Establishment

The establishment of Artificial Intelligence as a discipline that is clearly the foundation of today's discipline by that name occurred during the period from the famous 'Dartmouth Conference' of 1956 through the publication of the book *Computers and Thought* in 1963 (Feigenbaum & Feldman 1963).

Named and mostly organized by John McCarthy as "The Dartmouth Summer Research Project on Artificial Intelligence" the six-week long workshop brought together those who would establish and lead the major Artificial Intelligence research centers in North America for the next twenty years. McCarthy jointly established the MIT Artificial Intelligence Laboratory with Marvin Minsky, and then went on to found the

---

[8] Turing expresses his own belief that it will be possible for a machine with 10^9 bits of store to pass a five minute version of the test with 70% probability by about the year 2000.

[9] In fact there is a yearly competition with a $100,000 prize for a machine that can pass this version of the Turing test.

[10] An excerpt from Turing's paper is reprinted in Hofstadter & Dennett (1981). They leave out the whole section on learning and embodiment.

Stanford Artificial Intelligence Laboratory. Allen Newell and Herbert Simon shaped and lead the group that turned into the Computer Science department at Carnegie-Mellon University. Even today a large portion of the researchers in Artificial Intelligence in North America had one of these four people on their doctoral committee, or were advised by someone who did. The ideas expressed at the Dartmouth meeting have thus had a signal impact upon the field first named there.

As can be seen from interviews of the participants published in McCorduck (1979) there is still some disagreement over the intellectual property that was brought to the conference and its relative significance. The key outcome was the acceptance and rise of search as the pre-eminent tool of Artificial Intelligence. There was a general acceptance of the use of search to solve problems, and with this there was an essential abandonment of any notion of situatedness.

Minsky's earlier work had been involved with neural modeling. His Ph.D. thesis at Princeton was concerned with a model for the brain (Minsky 1954). Later, while at Harvard he was strongly influenced by McCulloch and Pitts (see McCulloch & Pitts (1943)), but by the time of the Dartmouth meeting he had become more involved with symbolic search-based systems. In his collection (Minsky 1968) of versions of his students' Ph.D. theses, all were concerned to some degree with defining and controlling an appropriate search space.

Simon and Newell presented their recent work on the *Logic Theorist* (Newell, Shaw & Simon 1957), a program that proved logic theorems by searching a tree of subgoals. The program made extensive use of heuristics to prune its search space. With this success, the idea of heuristic search soon became dominant within the still tiny Artificial Intelligence community.

McCarthy was not so affected by the conference that he had organized, and continues to this day to concentrate on epistemological issues rather than performance programs. However he was soon to invent the Lisp programming language (McCarthy 1960) which became the standard model of computation for Artificial Intelligence. It had great influence on the models of thought that were popular however, as it made certain things such as search, and representations based on individuals, much easier to program.

At the time, most programs were written in assembly language. It was a tedious job to write search procedures, especially recursive procedures in the machine languages of the day, although some people such as Samuel (1959) (another Dartmouth participant) were spectacularly successful. Newell and Simon owed much of their success in developing the Logic Theorist and their later General Problem Solver (Newell, Shaw & Simon 1959), to their use of an interpreted language (IPL-V—see

Newell, Shaw & Simon (1961)) which supported complex list structures and recursion. Many of their student's projects reported in Feigenbaum & Feldman (1963) also used this language.

McCarthy's Lisp was much cleaner and simpler. It made processing lists of information and recursive tree searches trivial to program–often a dozen lines of code could replace many hundreds of lines of assembler code. Search procedures now became even easier and more convenient to include in Artificial Intelligence programs. Lisp also had an influence on the classes of representational systems used, as is described in section 3.5.

In Minsky (1961), Artificial Intelligence was broken into five key topics: search, pattern recognition, learning, planning and induction. The second through fourth of these were characterized as ways of controlling search (respectively by better selection of tree expansion operators, by directing search through previous experience, and by replacing a given search with a smaller and more appropriate exploration). Again, most of the serious work in Artificial Intelligence according to this breakdown was concerned with search.

Eventually, after much experimentation (Michie & Ross 1970), search methods became well understood, formalized, and analyzed (Knuth & Moore 1975), and became celebrated as the primary method of Artificial Intelligence (Nilsson 1971).

At the end of the era of establishment, in 1963, Minsky generated an exhaustive annotated bibliography (Minsky 1963) of literature "directly concerned with construction of artificial problem-solving systems."[11] It contains 925 citations, 890 of which are to scientific papers and books, and 35 of which are to collections of such papers. There are two main points of interest here. First, although the title of the bibliography, "A Selected Descriptor-Indexed Bibliography to the Literature on Artificial Intelligence," refers to Artificial Intelligence, in his introduction he refers to the area of concern as "artificial problem-solving systems." Second, and somewhat paradoxically, the scope of the bibliography is much broader than one would expect from an AI bibliography today. It includes many items on cybernetics, neuroscience, bionics, information and communication theory, and first generation connectionism.

These two contrasting aspects of the bibliography highlight a trend in Artificial Intelligence that continued for the next 25 years. Out of a soup of ideas on how to build intelligent machines the disembodied and non-situated approach of problem-solving search systems emerged as dominant, at least within the community that referred to its own work as Artificial Intelligence.

---

[11] It also acted as the combined bibliography for the papers in Feigenbaum & Feldman (1963).

With hindsight we can step back and look at what happened. Originally search was introduced as a mechanism for solving problems that arguably humans used some search in solving. Chess and logic theorem proving are two examples we have already discussed. In these domains one does not expect instantaneous responses from humans doing the same tasks. They are not tasks that are situated in the world.

One can debate whether even in these tasks it is wise to rely so heavily on search, as bigger problems will have exponentially bad effects on search time—in fact Newell et al. (1958) argue just this, but produced a markedly slower chess program because of the complexity of static evaluation and search control. Some, such as Samuel (1959) with his checker's playing program, did worry about keeping things on a human timescale. Slagle (1963) in his symbolic integration program, was worried about being economically competitive with humans, but as he points out in the last two paragraphs of his paper, the explosive increase in price/performance ratio for computing was able to keep his programs ahead. In general, performance increases in computers were able to feed researchers with a steadily larger search space, enabling them to feel that they were making progress as the years went by. For any given technology level, a long-term freeze would soon show that programs relying on search had very serious problems, especially if there was any desire to situate them in a dynamic world.

In the last paragraph of Minsky (1961) he does bring up the possibility of a situated agent, acting as a "thinking aid" to a person. But again he relies on a performance increase in standard computing methods (this time through the introduction of time sharing) to supply the necessary time relevant computations.

In the early days of the formal discipline of Artificial Intelligence, search was adopted as a basic technology. It was easy to program on digital computers. It lead to reasoning systems which are not easy to shoe-horn into situated agents.

3.3   Cybernetics

There was, especially in the forties and fifties, another discipline which could be viewed as having the same goals as we have identified for Artificial Intelligence—the construction of useful intelligent systems and the understanding of human intelligence. This work, known as *Cybernetics*, had a fundamentally different flavor from the today's traditional Artificial Intelligence.

Cybernetics co-evolved with control theory and statistical information theory—e.g., see Wiener (1948) and Wiener (1961). It is the study of the mathematics of machines, not in terms of the functional components of a machine and how they are connected, and not in terms of what an individual machine can do here and now, and but rather in terms of *all* the possible behaviors that an individual machine can produce. There was a strong emphasis on characterizing a machine in terms of its inputs and outputs, and treating it as a *black box* as far as its internal workings were unobservable. The tools of analysis were often differential or integral equations, and these tools inherently limited cybernetics to situations where the boundary conditions were not changing rapidly. In contrast, they often do so in a system situated in a dynamically changing world—that complexity needs to go somewhere; either into discontinuous models or changed boundary conditions.

Cybernetics arose in the context of regulation of machinery and electronic circuits—it is often characterized by the subtitle of Wiener's book as the study of "control and communication in the animal and the machine". The model of computation at the time of its original development was analog. The inputs to and outputs from the machine to be analyzed were usually thought of as almost everywhere continuous functions with reasonable derivatives, and the mechanisms for automated analysis and modeling were usually things that today would be characterized as analog components. As such there was no notion of symbolic search—any search was couched in terms of minimization of a function. There was also much less of a notion of representation as an abstract manipulable entity than was found in the Artificial Intelligence approaches.

Much of the work in Cybernetics really was aimed at understanding animals and intelligence. Animals were modeled as machines, and from those models, it was hoped to glean how the animals changed their behavior through learning, and how that lead to better adaptation to the environment for the whole organism. It was recognized rather early (e.g., Ashby (1952) for an explicit statement) that an organism and its environment must be modeled together in order to understand the behavior produced by the organism—this is clearly an expression of situatedness. The tools of feedback analysis were used (Ashby 1956) to concentrate on such issues as stability of the system as the environment was perturbed, and in particular a system's *homeostasis* or ability to keep certain parameters within prescribed ranges, no matter what the uncontrolled variations within the environment.

With regards to embodiment there were some experiments along these lines. Many cybernetic models of organisms were rather abstract demonstrations of homeostasis, but some were concerned with physical robots. Walter (1950), Walter (1951), Walter (1953)[12] describes robots

---

[12] Much of the book Walter (1953) is concerned with early work on electroencephalography and hopes for its role in revealing the workings of the brain—forty years later these hopes do not seem to have been born out.

built on cybernetic principles which demonstrated goal-seeking behavior, homeostasis, and learning abilities.

The complexity and abilities of Walter's physically embodied machines rank with the purely imaginary ones in the first half dozen chapters of Braitenberg (1984) three decades later.

The limiting factors in these experiments were twofold; (1) the technology of building small self contained robots when the computational elements were miniature (a relative term) vacuum tubes, and (2) the lack of mechanisms for abstractly describing behavior at a level below the complete behavior, so that an implementation could reflect those simpler components. Thus in the first instance the models of thought were limited by technological barriers to implementing those models, and in the second instance, the lack of certain critical components of a model (organization into submodules) restricted the ability to build better technological implementations.

Let us return to Wiener and analyze the ways in which the mechanisms of cybernetics, and the mechanisms of computation were intimately interrelated in deep and self limiting ways.

Wiener was certainly aware of digital machines[13] even in his earlier edition of Wiener (1948). He compared them to analog machines such as the Bush differential analyzer, and declares that the digital (or *numerical*, as he called them) machines are superior for accurate numerical calculations. But in some deep sense Wiener did not see the flexibility of these machines. In an added chapter in Wiener (1961) he discussed the problem of building a self reproducing machine, and in the Cybernetic tradition, reduced the problem to modeling the input/output characteristics of a black box, in particular a non-linear transducer. He related methods for approximating observations of this function with a linear combination of basis non-linear transducers, and then showed that the whole problem could be done by summing and multiplying potentials and averaging over time. Rather than turn to a digital computer to do this he stated that there were some interesting possibilities for multiplication devices using piezo-electric effects. We see then the intimate tying together between models of computation, i.e., analog computation, and models of the essentials of self-reproduction. It is impossible to tease

---

[13] In the introduction to Wiener (1948) he talks about embodying such machines with photoelectric cells, thermometers, strain gauges and motors in the service of mechanical labor. But, in the text of the book he does not make such a connection with models of organisms. Rather he notes that they are intended for many successive runs, with the memory being cleared out between runs and states that "the brain, under normal circumstances, is not the complete analogue of the computing machine but rather the analogue of a single run on such a machine." His models of digital computation and models of thought are too dis-similar to make the connection that we would today.

apart cause and effect from this vantage point. The critical point is the way in which the mathematical proposal is tied to a technological implementation as a certification of the validity of the approach.[14]

By the mid sixties it was clear that the study of intelligence, even a study arising from the principles of cybernetics, if it was to succeed needed to be more broad-based in its levels of abstraction and tools of analysis. A good example is Arbib (1964).[15] Even so, he still harbors hope that cybernetic methods may turn out to give an understanding of the "overall coordinating and integrating principles" which interrelate the component subsystems of the human nervous system.

3.4   Abstraction

The years immediately following the Dartmouth conference shaped the field of Artificial Intelligence in a way which has not significantly changed. The next few years, in the main, amplified the abstraction away from situatedness, or connectedness to the world.[16] There were a number of demonstrations along the way which seemed to legitimize this abstraction. In this section I review some of those events, and argue that there were fundamental flaws in the conclusions generally drawn.

At MIT Roberts (1963) demonstrated a vision program that could match pre-stored models to visual images of blocks and wedges. This program was the forerunner of all modern vision programs, and it was many years before its performance could be matched by others. It took a grey level image of the world, and extracted a cartoon-like line drawing. It was this line drawing that was then fitted, via an inverse perspective transform to the pre-stored models. To those who saw its results this looked like a straightforward and natural way to process images and to build models (based on the prestored library) of the objective reality in front of the camera.

---

[14] With hindsight, an even wilder speculation is presented at the end of the later edition. Wiener suggests that the capital substances of genes and viruses may self reproduce through such a spectral analysis of infra-red emissions from the model molecules that then induce self organization into the undifferentiated magma of amino and nucleic acids available to form the new biological material.

[15] Arbib includes an elegant warning against being too committed to models, even mathematical models, which may turn out to be wrong. His statement that the "mere use of formulas gives no magical powers to a theory" is just as timely today as it was then.

[16] One exception was a computer controlled hand built at MIT, (Ernst 1961), and connected to the TX-0 computer. The hand was very much situated and embodied, and relied heavily on the external world as a model, rather than using internal representations. This piece of work seems to have gotten lost, for reasons that are not clear to me.

The unfortunate truth however, is that it is extra-ordinarily difficult to extract reliable line drawings in any sort of realistic cases of images. In Roberts' case the lighting was carefully controlled, the blocks were well painted, and the background was chosen with care. The images of his blocks produced rather complete line drawings with very little clutter where there should, by human observer standards, be no line elements. Today, after almost thirty years of research on bottom-up, top-down, and middle-out line finders, there is still no line finder that gets such clean results on a single natural image. Real world images are not at all the clean things that our personal introspection tells us they are. It is hard to appreciate this without working on an image yourself.[17]

The fallout of Roberts' program working on a very controlled set of images was that people thought that the line detection problem was doable and solved. E.g., Evans (1968) cites Roberts in his discussion of how input could obtained for his analogy program which compared sets of line drawings of 2-D geometric figures.

During the late sixties and early seventies the Shakey project (Nilsson 1984) at SRI reaffirmed the premises of abstract Artificial Intelligence. Shakey, mentioned in section 2, was a mobile robot that inhabited a set of specially prepared rooms. It navigated from room to room, trying to satisfy a goal given to it on a teletype. It would, depending on the goal and circumstances, navigate around obstacles consisting of large painted blocks and wedges, push them out of the way, or push them to some desired location.

Shakey had an onboard black and white television camera as its primary sensor. An offboard computer analyzed the images, and merged descriptions of what was seen into an existing first order predicate calculus model of the world. A planning program, STRIPS, operated on those symbolic descriptions of the world to generate a sequence of actions for Shakey. These plans were translated through a series of refinements into calls to atomic actions in fairly tight feedback loops with atomic sensing operations using Shakey's other sensors such as a bump bar and odometry.

Shakey was considered a great success at the time, demonstrating an integrated system involving mobility, perception, representation, planning, execution, and error recovery.

Shakey's success thus reaffirmed the idea of relying completely on internal models of an external objective reality. That is precisely the methodology it followed, and it appeared successful. However, it only worked because of very careful engineering of the environment. Twenty years later, no mobile robot has been demonstrated matching all aspects

---

[17] Try it! You'll be amazed at how bad it is.

of Shakey's performance in a more general environment, such as an office environment.

The rooms in which Shakey operated were bare except for the large colored blocks and wedges. This made the class of objects that had to be represented very simple. The walls were of a uniform color, and carefully lighted, with dark rubber baseboards, making clear boundaries with the lighter colored floor. This meant that very simple and robust vision of trihedral corners between two walls and the floor, could be used for relocalizing the robot in order to correct for drift in the robot's odometric measurements. The blocks and wedges were painted different colors on different planar surfaces. This ensured that it was relatively easy, especially in the good lighting provided, to find edges in the images separating the surfaces, and thus making it easy to identify the shape of the polyhedron. Blocks and wedges were relatively rare in the environment, eliminating problems due to partial obscurations. The objective reality of the environment was thus quite simple, and the mapping to an internal model of that reality was also quite plausible.

Around the same time at MIT a major demonstration was mounted of a robot which could view a scene consisting of stacked blocks, then build a copy of the scene using a robot arm (see Winston (1972)—the program was known as the *copy-demo*). The programs to do this were very specific to the blocks world, and would not have worked in the presence of simple curved objects, rough texture on the blocks, or without carefully controlled lighting. Nevertheless it reinforced the idea that a complete three dimensional description of the world could be extracted from a visual image. It legitimized the work of others, such as Winograd (1972), whose programs worked in a make-believe world of blocks—if one program could be built which understood such a world completely and could also manipulate that world, then it was assumed that programs which assumed that abstraction could in fact be connected to the real world without great difficulty. The problem remained of slowness of the programs due to the large search spaces, but as before, faster computers were always just around the corner.

The key problem that I see with all this work (apart from the use of search) is that it relied on the assumption that a complete world model could be built internally and then manipulated. The examples from Roberts, through Shakey and the copy-demo all relied on very simple worlds, and controlled situations. The programs were able to largely ignore unpleasant issues like sensor uncertainty, and were never really stressed because of the carefully controlled perceptual conditions. No computer vision systems can produce world models of this fidelity for anything nearing the complexity of realistic world scenes—even object recognition is an active and difficult research area. There are two responses to this: (1) eventually computer vision will catch up and provide such world models—I don't believe this based on the biological evidence presented below, or (2) complete objective models of reality are unrealistic—and hence the methods of Artificial Intelligence that rely on such models are unrealistic.

With the rise in abstraction it is interesting to note that it was still quite technologically difficult to connect to the real world for most Artificial Intelligence researchers.[18] For instance, Barrow & Salter (1970) describe efforts at Edinburgh, a major Artificial Intelligence center, to connect sensing to action, and the results are extraordinarily primitive by today's standards—both MIT and SRI had major engineering efforts in support of their successful activities. Moravec (1981) relates a sad tale of frustration from the early seventies of efforts at the Stanford Artificial Intelligence Laboratory to build a simple mobile robot with visual input.

Around the late sixties and early seventies there was a dramatic increase in the availability of computer processing power available to researchers at reasonably well equipped laboratories. Not only was there a large increase in processing speed and physical memory, but time sharing systems became well established. An individual researcher was now able to work continuously and conveniently on a disembodied program designed to exhibit intelligence. However, connections to the real world were not only difficult and overly expensive, but the physical constraints of using them made development of the 'intelligent' parts of the system slower by at least an order of magnitude, and probably two orders, as compared to the new found power of timesharing. The computers clearly had a potential to influence the models of thought used—and certainly that hypothesis is not contradicted by the sort of micro-world work that actually went on.

3.5 Knowledge

By this point in the history of Artificial Intelligence, the trends, assumptions, and approaches had become well established. The last fifteen years have seen the discipline thundering along on inertia more than anything else. Apart from a renewed flirtation with neural models (see section 3.8 below) there has been very little change in the underlying assumptions about the models of thought. This coincides with an era of very little technical innovation in our underlying models of computation.

---

[18] It is still fairly difficult even today. There are very few turnkey systems available for purchase which connect sensors to reasonable computers, and reasonable computers to actuators. The situation does seem to be rapidly improving however—we may well be just about to step over a significant threshold.

For the remainder of section 3, I rather briefly review the progress made over the last fifteen years, and show how it relates to the fundamental issues of situatedness and embodiment brought up earlier.

One problem with micro-worlds is that they are somewhat uninteresting. The blocks world was the most popular micro-world and there is very little that can be done in it other than make stacks of blocks. After a flurry of early work where particularly difficult 'problems' or 'puzzles' were discovered and then solved (e.g., Sussman (1975)) it became more and more difficult to do something new within that domain.

There were three classes of responses to this impoverished problem space:

- Move to other domains with equally simple semantics, but with more interesting print names than *block-a* etc. It was usually not the intent of the researchers to do this, but many in fact did fall into this trap. Winograd & Flores (1986) expose and criticize a number of such dressings up in the chapter on "Understanding Language".

- Build a more complex semantics into the blocks world and work on the new problems which arise. A rather heroic example of this is Fahlman (1974) who included balance, multi-shaped blocks, friction, and the like. The problem with this approach is that the solutions to the 'puzzles' become so domain specific that it is hard to see how they might generalize to other domains.

- Move to the wider world. In particular, represent knowledge about the everyday world, and then build problem solvers, learning systems, etc., that operate in this semantically richer world.

The last of these approaches has spawned possibly the largest recognizable subfield of Artificial Intelligence, known as Knowledge Representation. It has its own conferences. It has theoretical and practical camps. Yet, it is totally ungrounded. It concentrates much of its energies on anomalies within formal systems which are never used for any practical tasks.

Brachman & Levesque (1985) is a collection of papers in the area. The knowledge representation systems described receive their input either in symbolic form or as the output of natural language systems. The goal of the papers seems to be to represent 'knowledge' about the world. However it is totally ungrounded. There is very little attempt to use the knowledge (save in the naive physics (Hayes 1985), or qualitative physics (de Kleer & Brown 1984) areas—but note that these areas too are ungrounded). There is an implicit assumption that someday the inputs and outputs will be connected to something which will make use of them (see Brooks (1991c) for an earlier criticism of this approach).

In the meantime the work proceeds with very little to steer it, and much of it concerns problems produced by rather simple-minded attempts at representing complex concepts. To take but one example, there have been many pages written on the problem of penguins being birds, even though they cannot fly. The reason that this is a problem is that the knowledge representation systems are built on top of a computational technology that makes convenient the use of very simple individuals (Lisp atoms) and placing links between them. As pointed out in Brooks (1990c), and much earlier in Brooks (1991c), such a simple approach does not work when the system is to be physically grounded through embodiment. It seems pointless to try to patch up a system which in the long run cannot possibly work. Dreyfus (1981)[19] provides a useful criticism of this style of work.

Perhaps the pinnacle of the knowledge-is-everything approach can be found in Lenat & Feigenbaum (1991) where they discuss the foundations of a 10-year project to encode knowledge having the scope of a simple encyclopedia. It is a totally unsituated, and totally disembodied approach. Everything the system is to know is through hand-entered units of 'knowledge', although there is some hope expressed that later it will be able to learn itself by reading. Smith (1991) provides a commentary on this approach, and points out how the early years of the project have been devoted to finding a more primitive level of knowledge than was previously envisioned for grounding the higher levels of knowledge. It is my opinion, and also Smith's, that there is a fundamental problem still and one can expect continued regress until the system has some form of embodiment.

3.6   Robotics

Section 2 outlined the early history of mobile robots. There have been some interesting developments over the last ten years as attempts have been made to embody some theories from Artificial Intelligence in mobile robots. In this section I briefly review some of the results.

In the early eighties the Defense Advanced Research Projects Agency (DARPA) in the US, sponsored a major thrust in building an Autonomous Land Vehicle. The initial task for the vehicle was to run along a paved road in daylight using vision as the primary perceptual sense. The first attempts at this problem (e.g., Waxman, Moigne & Srinivasan

---

[19]Endorsement of some of Dreyfus' views should not be taken as whole hearted embrace of all his arguments.

(1985)) followed the SMPA methodology. The idea was to build a three-dimensional world model of the road ahead, then plan a path along it, including steering and velocity control annotations. These approaches failed as it was not possible to recover accurate three-dimensional road models from the visual images. Even under fairly strong assumptions about the class of roads being followed the programs would produce ludicrously wrong results.

With the pressure of getting actual demonstrations of the vehicle running on roads, and of having all the processing onboard, radical changes had to made in the approaches taken. Two separate teams came up with similar approaches, Turk, Morgenthaler, Gremban & Marra (1988) at Martin Marietta, the integrating contractor, and Thorpe, Herbert, Kanade & Shafer (1988) at CMU, the main academic participant in the project, both producing vision-based navigation systems. Both systems operated in picture coordinates rather than world coordinates, and both successfully drove vehicles along the roads. Neither system generated three dimensional world models. Rather, both identified road regions in the images and servo-ed the vehicle to stay on the road. The systems can be characterized as reactive, situated and embodied. Horswill & Brooks (1988) describe a system of similar vintage which operates an indoor mobile robot under visual navigation. The shift in approach taken on the outdoor vehicle was necessitated by the realities of the technology available, and the need to get things operational.

Despite these lessons there is still a strong bias to following the traditional Artificial Intelligence SMPA approach as can be seen in the work at CMU on the Ambler project. The same team that adopted a reactive approach to the road following problem have reverted to a cumbersome, complex, and slow complete world modeling approach (Simmons & Krotkov 1991).

3.7   Vision

Inspired by the work of Roberts (1963) and that on Shakey (Nilsson 1984), the vision community has been content to work on scene description problems for many years. The implicit intent has been that when the reasoning systems of Artificial Intelligence were ready, the vision systems would be ready to deliver world models as required, and the two could be hooked together to get a situated, or embodied system.

There are numerous problems with this approach, and too little room to treat them adequately within the space constraints of this paper. The fundamental issue is that Artificial Intelligence and Computer Vision have made an assumption that the purpose of vision is to reconstruct the static external world (for dynamic worlds it is just supposed to do it often and quickly) as a three dimensional world model. I do not believe that this is possible with the generality that is usually assumed. Furthermore I do not think it is necessary, nor do I think that it is what human vision does. Section 4 discusses some of these issues a little more.

3.8   Parallelism

Parallel computers are potentially quite different from Von Neumann machines. One might expect then that parallel models of computation would lead to fundamentally different models of thought. The story about parallelism, and the influence of parallel machines on models of thought, and the influence of models of thought on parallel machines has two and a half pieces. The first piece arose around the time of the early cybernetics work, the second piece exploded in the mid-eighties and we have still to see all the casualties. The last half piece has been pressured by the current models of thought to change the model of parallelism.

There was a large flurry of work in the late fifties and sixties involving linear threshold devices, commonly known as perceptrons. The extremes in this work are represented by Rosenblatt (1962) and Minsky & Papert (1969). These devices were used in rough analogy to neurons and were to be wired into networks that learned to do some task, rather than having to be programmed. Adjusting the weights on the inputs of these devices was roughly equivalent in the model to adjusting the synaptic weights where axons connect to dendrites in real neurons— this is currently considered as the likely site of most learning within the brain.

The idea was that the network had specially distinguished inputs and outputs. Members of classes of patterns would be presented to the inputs and the outputs would be given a correct classification. The difference between the correct response and the actual response of the network would then be used to update weights on the inputs of individual devices. The key driving force behind the blossoming of this field was the perceptron convergence theorem that showed that a simple parameter adjustment technique would always let a single perceptron learn a discrimination if there existed a set of weights capable of making that discrimination.

To make things more manageable the networks were often structured as layers of devices with connections only between adjacent layers. The directions of the connections were strictly controlled, so that there were no feedback loops in the network and that there was a natural progression from one single layer that would then be the input layer, and one layer would be the output layer. The problem with multi-layer networks was that there was no obvious way to assign the credit or blame over the layers for a correct or incorrect pattern classification.

In the formal analyses that were carried out (e.g., Nilsson (1965) and Minsky & Papert (1969)) only a single layer of devices which could learn, or be adjusted, were ever considered. Nilsson (1965) in the later chapters did consider multi-layer machines, but in each case, all but one layer consisted of static unmodifiable devices. There was very little work on analyzing machines with feedback.

None of these machines was particularly situated, or embodied. They were usually tested on problems set up by the researcher. There were many abuses of the scientific method in these tests—the results were not always as the researchers interpreted them.

After the publication of Minsky & Papert (1969), which contained many negative results on the capabilities of single layer machines, the field seemed to die out for about fifteen years.

Recently there has been a resurgence in the field starting with the publication of Rumelhart & McClelland (1986).

The new approaches were inspired by a new learning algorithm known as *back propagation* (Rumelhart, Hinton & Williams 1986). This algorithm gives a method for assigning credit and blame in fully connected multi-layer machines without feedback loops. The individual devices within the layers have linearly weighted inputs and a differentiable output function, a sigmoid, which closely matches a step function, or threshold function. Thus they are only slight generalizations of the earlier perceptrons, but their continuous and differentiable outputs enable hill climbing to be performed which lets the networks converge eventually to be able to classify inputs appropriately as trained.

Back propagation has a number of problems; it is slow to learn in general, and there is a learning rate which needs to be tuned by hand in most cases. The effect of a low learning rate is that the network might often get stuck in local minima. The effect of a higher learning rate is that the network may never really converge as it will be able to jump out of the correct minimum as well as it can jump out of an incorrect minimum. These problems combine to make back propagation, which is the cornerstone of modern neural network research, inconvenient for use in embodied or situated systems.

In fact, most of the examples in the new wave of neural networks have not been situated or embodied. There are a few counterexamples (e.g., Sejnowski & Rosenberg (1987), Atkeson (1989) and Viola (1990)) but in the main they are not based on back propagation. The most successful recent learning techniques for situated, embodied, mobile robots, have not been based on parallel algorithms at all—rather they use a reinforcement learning algorithm such as Q-learning (Watkins 1989) as for example, Kaelbling (1990) and Mahadevan & Connell (1990).

One problem for neural networks becoming situated or embodied is that they do not have a simple translation into time varying perception or action pattern systems. They need extensive front and back ends to equip them to interact with the world—all the cited examples above had such features added to them.

Both waves of neural network research have been heralded by predictions of the demise of all other forms of computation. It has not happened in either case. Both times there has been a bandwagon effect where many people have tried to use the mechanisms that have become available to solve many classes of problems, often without regard to whether the problems could even be solved in principle by the methods used. In both cases the enthusiasm for the approach has been largely stimulated by a single piece of technology, first the perceptron training rule, and then the back propagation algorithm.

And now for the last half-piece of the parallel computation story. The primary hope for parallel computation helping Artificial Intelligence has been the Connection Machine developed by Hillis (1985). This is a SIMD machine, and as such might be thought to have limited applicability for general intelligent activities. Hillis, however, made a convincing case that it could be used for many algorithms having to do with knowledge representation, and that it would speed them up, often to be constant time algorithms. The book describing the approach is exciting, and in fact on pages 4 and 5 of Hillis (1985) the author promises to break the Von Neumann bottleneck by making all the silicon in a machine actively compute all the time. The argument is presented that most of the silicon in a Von Neumann machine is devoted to memory, and most of that is inactive most of the time. This was a brave new approach, but it has not survived the market place. New models of the connection machine have large local memories (in the order of 64K bits) associated with each one bit processor (there can be up to 64K processors in a single Connection Machine). Once again, most of the silicon is inactive most of the time. Connection machines are used within Artificial Intelligence laboratories mostly for computer vision where there is an obvious mapping from processors and their NEWS network to pixels of standard digital images. Traditional Artificial Intelligence approaches are so tied to their traditional machine architectures that they have been hard to map to this new sort of architecture.

4   Biology

We have our own introspection to tell us how our minds work, and
our own observations to tell us how the behavior of other people and
of animals works. We have our own partial theories and methods of
explanation.[20] Sometimes, when an observation, internal or external,
does not fit our pre-conceptions, we are rather ready to dismiss it as
something we do not understand, and do not need to understand.

In this section I will skim over a scattering of recent work from ethology, psychology, and neuroscience, in an effort to indicate how deficient
our everyday understanding of behavior really is. This is important to
realize because traditional Artificial Intelligence has relied at the very
least implicitly, and sometimes quite explicitly, on these folk understand-
ings of human and animal behavior. The most common example is the
story about getting from Boston to California (or vice-versa), which sets
up an analogy between what a person does mentally in order to *Plan*
the trip, and the means-ends method of planning. See Agre (1991) for
a more detailed analysis of the phenomenon.

4.1   Ethology

Ethology, the study of animal behavior, tries to explain the causation,
development, survival value, and evolution of behavior patterns within
animals. See McFarland (1985) for an easy introduction to modern
ethology.

Perhaps the most famous ethologist was Niko Tinbergen (closely followed by his co-Nobel winners Konrad Lorenz and Karl von Frisch). His
heirarchical view of intelligence, described in Tinbergen (1951), is often quoted by Artificial Intelligence researchers in support of their own
hierarchical theories. However, this approach was meant to be a neu-
robiologically plausible theory, but it was described in the absence any
evidence. Tinbergen's model has largely been replaced in modern ethology by theories of motivational competition, disinhibition, and dominant
and sub-dominant behaviors.

There is no completely worked out theory of exactly how the decision is made as to which behavioral pattern (e.g., drinking or eating)
should be active in an animal. A large number of experiments give evidence of complex internal and external feedback loops in determining
an appropriate behavior. McFarland (1988) presents a number of such
experiments and demonstrates the challenges for the theories. The experimental data has ruled out the earlier hierarchical models of behavior

---

[20] See Churchland (1986) for a discussion of folk psychology.

selection, and current theories share many common properties with the behavior-based approach advocated in this paper.

4.2   Psychology

The way in which our brains work is quite hidden from us. We have some introspection, we believe, to some aspects of our thought processes, but there are certainly perceptual and motor areas that we are quite confident we have no access to.[21] To tease out the mechanisms at work we can do at least two sorts of experiments: we can test the brain at limits of its operational envelop to see how it breaks down, and we can study damaged brains and get a glimpse at the operation of previously integrated components. In fact, some of these observations call into question the reliability of any of our own introspections.

There have been many psychophysical experiments to test the limits of human visual perception. We are all aware of so-called *optical illusions* where our visual apparatus seems to break down. The journal *Perception* regularly carries papers which show that what we perceive is not what we see (e.g., Ramachandran & Anstis (1985)). For instance in visual images of a jumping leopard whose spots are made to artificially move about, we perceive them all as individually following the leopard. The straightforward model of human perception proposed by Marr (1982), and almost universally accepted by Artificial Intelligence vision researchers, does not account for such results. Likewise it is now clear that the color pathway is separate from the intensity pathway in the human visual system, and our color vision is something of an illusion.[22] We are unaware of these deficiencies—most people are not aware that they have a blind spot in each eye the size of the image of the moon—they are totally inaccessible to our consciousness. Even more surprising, our very notion of consciousness is full of inconsistencies—psychophysical experiments show that our experience of the flow of time as we observe things in the world is an illusion, as we can often consciously perceive things in a temporal order inconsistent with the world as constructed by an experimenter (see Dennett & Kinsbourne (1990) for an overview).

We turn now to damaged brains to get a glimpse at how things might be organized. This work can better be termed *neuropsychology*. There is a large body of literature on this subject from which we merely pick out just a few instances here. The purpose is to highlight the fact that the

---

[21] This contrasts with a popular fad in Artificial Intelligence where all reasoning of a system is supposed to be available to a meta-reasoning system, or even introspectively to the system itself.

[22] See the techniques used in the current trend of 'colorization' of black and white movie classics for a commercial capitalization on our visual deficiencies.

approaches taken in traditional Artificial Intelligence are vastly different from the way the human brain is organized.

The common view in Artificial Intelligence, and particularly in the knowledge representation community, is that there is a central storage system which links together the information about concepts, individuals, categories, goals, intentions, desires, and whatever else might be needed by the system. In particular there is a tendency to believe that the knowledge is stored in a way that is independent from the way or circumstances in which it was acquired.

McCarthy & Warrington (1988) (and a series of earlier papers by them and their colleagues) give cause to doubt this seemingly logical organization. They report on a particular individual (identified as TOB), who at an advanced age developed a semantic deficit in knowledge of living things, but retained a reasonable knowledge of inanimate things. By itself, this sounds perfectly plausible—the semantic knowledge might just be stored in a category specific way, and the animate part of the storage has been damaged. But, it happens that TOB is able to access the knowledge when, for example he was shown a picture of a dolphin— he was able to form sentences using the word 'dolphin' and talk about its habitat, its ability to be trained, and its role in the US military. When verbaly alsked what a dolphin is, however, he thought it was either a fish or a bird. He has no such conflict in knowledge when the subject is a wheelbarrow, say. The authors argue that since the deficit is not complete but shows degradation, the hypothesis that there is a deficit in a particular type of sensory modality access to a particular category subclass in a single database is not valid. Through a series of further observations they argue that they have shown evidence of modality-specific organization of meaning, besides a category specific organization. Thus knowledge may be duplicated in many places, and may by no means be uniformly accessible. There are examples of where the knowledge is shown to be inconsistent. Our normal introspection does not reveal this organization, and would seem to be at odds with these explanations. Below, we call into question our normal introspection.

Newcombe & Ratcliff (1989) present a long discussion of visuospatial disorders in brain damaged patients. Many of these severely tax the model of a person as an integrated rational agent. One simple example they report is finger agnosia, where a patient may be quite impaired in the way he can carry out conscious simple tasks using their fingers, but could still do things such as thread a needle, or play the piano well. This suggests the existence of multiple parallel channels of control, rather than some centralized finger control box, for instance.

Teitelbaum, Pellis & Pellis (1990) summarize work which shows that rat locomotion involves a number of reflexes. Drugs can be used to shut off many reflexes so that a rat will appear to be unable to move. Almost all stimuli have no effect—the rat simply remains with its limbs in whatever configuration the experimenter has arranged them. However certain very specific stimuli can trigger a whole chain of complex motor interactions—e.g., tilting the surface on which the rats feet are resting to the point where the rat starts to slide will cause the rat to leap. There has also been a recent popularization of the work of Sacks (1974) which shows similar symptoms, in somewhat less understood detail, for humans. Again, it is hard to explain these results in terms of a centralized will—rather an interpretation of multiple almost independent agencies such as hypothesized by Minsky (1986) seems a better explanation.

Perhaps the most remarkable sets of results are from split brain patients. It has become common knowledge that we all possess a left brain and a right brain, but in patients whose *corpus callosum* has been severed they really do become separate operational brains in their own rights (Gazzaniga & LeDoux 1977).

Through careful experimentation it is possible to independently communicate with the two brains, visually with both, and verbally with the left. By setting up experiments where one side does not have access to the information possessed by the other side, it is possible to push hard on the introspection mechanisms. It turns out that the ignorant half prefers to fabricate explanations for what is going on, rather than admit ignorance. These are normal people (except their brains are cut in half), and it seems that they sincerely believe the lies they are telling, as a result of confabulations generated during introspection. One must question then the ordinary introspection that goes on when our brains are intact.

What is the point of all this? The traditional Artificial Intelligence model of representation and organization along centralized lines is not how people are built. Traditional Artificial Intelligence methods are certainly not necessary for intelligence then, and so far they have not really been demonstrated to be sufficient in situated, embodied systems. The organization of humans is by definition sufficient—it is not known at all whether it will turn out to be necessary. The point is that we cannot make assumptions of necessity under either approach. The best we can expect to do for a while at least, is to show that some approach is sufficient to produce interesting intelligence.

4.3 Neuroscience

The working understanding of the brain among Artificial Intelligence researchers seems to be that it is an electrical machine with electrical inputs and outputs to the sensors and actuators of the body. One can see this assumption made explicit, for example, in the fiction and speculative writing of professional Artificial Intelligence researchers such as Hofstadter & Dennett (1981) and Moravec (1988). This view, and further reduction, leads to the very simple models of brain used in connectionism (Rumelhart & McClelland 1986).

In fact, however, the brain is embodied with a much more serious coupling. The brain is situated in a soup of hormones, that influences it in the strongest possible ways. It receives messages encoded hormonally, and sends messages so encoded throughout the body. Our electrocentrism, based on our electronic models of computation, has lead us to ignore these aspects in our informal models of neuroscience, but hormones play a strong, almost dominating, role in determination of behavior in both simple (Kravitz 1988) and higher animals (Bloom 1976).[23]

Real biological systems are not rational agents that take inputs, compute logically, and produce outputs. They are a mess of many mechanisms working in various ways, out of which emerges the behavior that we observe and rationalize. We can see this in more detail by looking both at the individual computational level, and at the organizational level of the brain.

We do not really know how computation is done at the lowest levels in the brain. There is debate over whether the neuron is the functional unit of the nervous system, or whether a single neuron can act as a many independent smaller units (Cohen & Wu 1990). However, we do know that signals are propagated along axons and dendrites at very low speeds compared to electronic computers, and that there are significant delays crossing synapses. The usual estimates for the computational speed of neuronal systems are no more than about 1 KiloHertz. This implies that the computations that go on in humans to effect actions in the subsecond range must go through only a very limited number of processing steps—the network cannot be very deep in order to get meaningful results out on the timescales that routinely occur for much of human thought. On the other hand, the networks seem incredibly richly connected, compared to the connection width of either our electronic systems, or our connectionist models. For simple creatures some motor neurons are connected to tens of percent of the other neurons in the animal. For mammals motor neurons are typically connected to 5,000 and some neurons in humans are connected to as many as 90,000 other neurons (Churchland 1986).

---

[23] See Bergland (1985) for a history of theories of the brain, and how they were influenced by the current technologies available to provide explanatory power. Unfortunately this book is marred by the author's own lack of understanding of computation which leads him to dismiss electrical activity of the brain as largely irrelevant to the process of thought.

For one very simple animal *Caenorhabditis elegans*, a nematode, we have a complete wiring diagram of its nervous system, including its development stages (Wood 1988). In the hermaphrodite there are 302 neurons and 56 support cells out of the animal's total of 959 cells. In the male there are 381 neurons and 92 support cells out of a total of 1031 cells. Even though the anatomy and behavior of this creature are well studied, and the neuronal activity is well probed, the way in which the circuits control the animal's behavior is not understood very well at all.

Given that even a simple animal is not yet understood one cannot expect to gain complete insight into building Artificial Intelligence by looking at the nervous systems of complex animals. We can, however, get insight into aspects of intelligent behavior, and some clues about sensory systems and motor systems.

Wehner (1987) for instance, gives great insight into the way in which evolution has selected for sensor-neurological couplings with the environment which can be very specialized. By choosing the right sensors, animals can often get by with very little neurological processing, in order to extract just the right information about the here and now around them, for the task at hand. Complex world model building is not possible given the sensors' limitations, and not needed when the creature is appropriately situated.

Cruse (1990) and Götz & Wenking (1973) give insight into how simple animals work, based on an understanding at a primitive level of their neurological circuits. These sorts of clues can help us as we try to build walking robots–for examples of such computational neuroethology see Brooks (1989) and Beer (1990).

These clues can help us build better artificial systems, but by themselves they do not provide us with a full theory.

5   Ideas

Earlier we identified situatedness, embodiment, intelligence, and emergence, with a set of key ideas that have lead to a new style of Artificial Intelligence research which we are calling behavior-based robots. In this section I expound on these four topics in more detail.

5.1   Situatedness

Traditional Artificial Intelligence has adopted a style of research where the agents that are built to test theories in intelligence are essentially problem solvers that work in an symbolic abstracted domain. The symbols may have referents in the minds of the builders of the systems, but there is nothing to ground those referents in any real world. Furthermore, the agents are not situated in a world at all. Rather they are given a problem, and they solve it. Then, they are given another problem and they solve it. They are not participating in a world as would agents in the usual sense.

In these systems there is no external world per se, with continuity, surprises, or ongoing history. The programs deal only with a model world, with its own built-in physics. There is a blurring between the knowledge of the agent and the world it is supposed to be operating in—indeed in many Artificial Intelligence systems there is no distinction between the two—the agent has access to direct and perfect perception, and direct and perfect action. When consideration is given to porting such agents or systems to operate in the world, the question arises of what sort of representation they need of the real world. Over the years within traditional Artificial Intelligence, it has become accepted that they will need an objective model of the world with individuated entities, tracked and identified over time—the models of knowledge representation that have been developed expect and require such a one-to-one correspondence between the world and the agent's representation of it.

The early robots such as Shakey and the Cart certainly followed this approach. They built models of the world, planned paths around obstacles, and updated their estimate of where objects were relative to themselves as they moved. We developed a different approach (Brooks 1986) where a mobile robot used the world as its own model—continuously referring to its sensors rather than to an internal world model. The problems of object class and identity disappeared. The perceptual processing became much simpler. And the performance of the robot was better in comparable tasks than that of the Cart,[24] and with much less computation, even allowing for the different sensing modalities.

Agre (1988) and Chapman (1990) formalized these ideas in their arguments for *deictic* (or *indexical-functional* in an earlier incarnation) representations. Instead of having representations of individual entities in the world, the system has representations in terms of the relationship of the entities to the robot. These relationships are both spatial and functional. For instance in Pengi (Agre & Chapman 1987), rather than refer to *Bee-27* the system refers to *the-bee-that-is-chasing-me-now*. The latter may or may not be the same bee that was chasing the robot two minutes previously—it doesn't matter for the particular tasks in which the robot is engaged.

---

[24] The tasks carried out by this first robot, *Allen*, were of a different class than those attempted by Shakey. Shakey could certainly not have carried out the tasks that Allen did.

When this style of representation is used it is possible to build computational systems which trade off computational depth for computational width. The idea is that the computation can be represented by a network of gates, timers, and state elements. The network does not need long paths from inputs (sensors) to outputs (actuators). Any computation that is capable of being done is done in a very short time span. There have been other approaches which address a similar time-bounded computation issue, namely the *bounded rationality* approach (Russell 1989). Those approaches try to squeeze a traditional Artificial Intelligence system into a bounded amount of computation. With the new approach we tend to come from the other direction, we start with very little computation and build up the amount, while staying away from the boundary of computation that takes too long. As more computation needs to be added there is a tendency to add it in breadth (thinking of the computation as being represented by a circuit whose depth is the longest path length in gates from input to output) rather than depth.

A situated agent must respond in a timely fashion to its inputs. Modeling the world completely under these conditions can be computationally challenging. But a world in which it is situated also provides some continuity to the agent. That continuity can be relied upon, so that the agent can use its perception of the world instead of an objective world model. The representational primitives that are useful then change quite dramatically from those in traditional Artificial Intelligence.

The key idea from situatedness is:

The world is its own best model.

5.2   Embodiment

There are two reasons that embodiment of intelligent systems is critical. First, only an embodied intelligent agent is fully validated as one that can deal with the real world. Second, only through a physical grounding can any internal symbolic or other system find a place to bottom out, and give 'meaning' to the processing going on within the system.

The physical grounding of a robot in the world forces its designer to deal with all the issues. If the intelligent agent has a body, has sensors, and has actuators, then all the details and issues of being in the world must be faced. It is no longer possible to argue in conference papers, that the simulated perceptual system is realistic, or that problems of uncertainty in action will not be significant. Instead, physical experiments can be done simply and repeatedly. There is no room for cheating.[25]

---

[25] I mean this in the sense of causing self-delusion, not in the sense of wrong doing with intent.

When this is done it is usual to find that many of the problems that seemed significant are not so in the physical system (typically 'puzzle' like situations where symbolic reasoning seemed necessary tend not to arise in embodied systems), and many that seemed non-problems become major hurdles (typically these concern aspects of perception and action).[26]

A deeper problem is "can there be disembodied mind?". Many believe that what is human about us is very directly related to our physical experiences. For instance Johnson (1987) argues that a large amount of our language is actually metaphorically related to our physical connections to the world. Our mental 'concepts' are based on physically experienced exemplars. Smith (1991) suggests that without physical grounding there can be no halt to the regress within a knowledge based system as it tries to reason about real world knowledge such as that contained in an encyclopedia (e.g., Lenat & Feigenbaum (1991)).

Without an ongoing participation and perception of the world there is no meaning for an agent. Everything is random symbols. Arguments might be made that at some level of abstraction even the human mind operates in this solipsist position. However, biological evidence (see section 4) suggests that the human mind's connection to the world is so strong, and many faceted, that these philosophical abstractions may not be correct.

The key idea from embodiment is:

The world grounds regress.

5.3   Intelligence

Brooks (1991c) argues that the sorts of activities we usually think of as demonstrating intelligence in humans have been taking place for only a very small fraction of our evolutionary lineage. Further, I argue that the 'simple' things to do with perception and mobility in a dynamic environment took evolution much longer to perfect, and that all those capabilities are a necessary basis for 'higher-level' intellect.

Therefore, I proposed looking at simpler animals as a bottom-up model for building intelligence. It is soon apparent, when 'reasoning' is stripped away as the prime component of a robot's intellect, that the

---

[26] In fact, there is some room for cheating as the physical environment can be specially simplified for the robot—and in fact it may be very hard in some cases to identify such self delusions. In some research projects it may be necessary to test a particular class of robot activities, and therefore it may be necessary to build a test environment for the robot. There is a fine and difficult to define line to be drawn here.

dynamics of the interaction of the robot and its environment are primary determinants of the structure of its intelligence.

Earlier, Simon (1969) had discussed a similar point in terms of an ant walking along the beach. He pointed out that the complexity of the behavior of the ant is more a reflection of the complexity of its environment than its own internal complexity. He speculated that the same may be true of humans, but within two pages of text had reduced studying human behavior to the domain of crypto-arithmetic problems.

It is hard to draw the line at what is intelligence, and what is environmental interaction. In a sense it does not really matter which is which, as all intelligent systems must be situated in some world or other if they are to be useful entities.

The key idea from intelligence is:

> *Intelligence is determined by the dynamics of interaction with the world.*

5.4   Emergence

In discussing where intelligence resides in an Artificial Intelligence program Minsky (1961) points out that "there is never any 'heart' in a program" and "we find senseless loops and sequences of trivial operations". It is hard to point at a single component as the seat of intelligence. There is no homunculus. Rather, intelligence emerges from the interaction of the components of the system. The way in which it emerges, however, is quite different for traditional and behavior-based Artificial Intelligence systems.

In traditional Artificial Intelligence the modules that are defined are information processing, or functional. Typically these modules might be a perception module, a planner, a world modeler, a learner, etc. The components directly participate in functions such as perceiving, planning, modeling, learning, etc. Intelligent behavior of the system, such as avoiding obstacles, standing up, controlling gaze, etc., emerges from the interaction of the components.

In behavior-based Artificial Intelligence the modules that are defined are behavior producing. Typically these modules might be an obstacle avoidance behavior, a standing up behavior, a gaze control behavior, etc. The components directly participate in producing behaviors such as avoiding obstacles, standing up, controlling gaze, etc. Intelligent functionality of the system, such as perception, planning, modeling, learning, etc., emerges from the interaction of the components.

Although this dualism between traditional and behavior-based systems looks pretty it is not completely accurate. Traditional systems have hardly ever been really connected to the world, and so the emergence of intelligent behavior is something more of an expectation in most cases, rather than an established phenomenon. Conversely, because of the many behaviors present in a behavior-based system, and their individual dynamics of interaction with the world, it is often hard to say that a particular series of actions was produced by a particular behavior. Sometimes many behaviors are operating simultaneously, or are switching rapidly (Horswill & Brooks 1988).

Over the years there has been a lot of work on emergence based on the theme of self-organization (e.g., Nicolis & Prigogine (1977)). Within behavior-based robots there is beginning to be work at better characterizing emergent functionality, but it is still in its early stages, e.g., Steels (1990). He defines it as meaning that a function is achieved "indirectly by the interaction of more primitive components among themselves and with the world".

It is hard to identify the seat of intelligence within any system, as intelligence is produced by the interactions of many components. Intelligence can only be determined by the total behavior of the system and how that behavior appears in relation to the environment.

The key idea from emergence is:

> *Intelligence is in the eye of the observer.*

6   Thought

Since late 1984 I have been building autonomous mobile robots in the 'Mobot Lab' at the MIT Artificial Intelligence Laboratory; Brooks (1986) gives the original ideas, and Brooks (1990c) contains a recent summary of the capabilities of the robots developed in my laboratory over the years.

My work fits within the framework described above in terms of situatedness, embodiment, intelligence and emergence. In particular I have advocated situatedness, embodiment, and highly reactive architectures with no reasoning systems, no manipulable representations, no symbols, and totally decentralized computation. This different model of computation has lead to radically different models of thought.

I have been accused of overstating the case that the new approach is all that is necessary to build truly intelligent systems. It has even been suggested that as an evangelist I have deliberately overstated my case to pull people towards the correct level of belief, and that really all along, I have known that a hybrid approach is necessary.

That is not what I believe. I think that the new approach can be extended to cover the whole story, both with regards to building intelligent systems and to understanding human intelligence—the two principal goals identified for Artificial Intelligence at the beginning of the paper.

Whether I am right or not is an empirical question. Multiple approaches to Artificial Intelligence will continue to be pursued. At some point we will be able to evaluate which approach has been more successful.

In this section I want to outline the philosophical underpinnings of my work, and discuss why I believe the approach is the one that will in the end will prove dominant.

6.1   Principles

All research goes on within the constraints of certain principles. Sometimes these are explicit, and sometimes they are implicit. In the following paragraphs I outline as explicitly as I can the principles followed.

The first set of principles defines the domain for the work.

- The goal is to study complete integrated intelligent autonomous agents.

- The agents should be embodied as mobile robots, situated in unmodified worlds found around our laboratory.[27] This confronts the embodiment issue. The environments chosen are for convenience, although we strongly resist the temptation to change the environments in any way for the robots.

- The robots should operate equally well when visitors, or cleaners, walk through their workspace, when furniture is rearranged, when lighting or other environmental conditions change, and when their sensors and actuators drift in calibration. This confronts the situatedness issue.

- The robots should operate on timescales commensurate with the time scales used by humans. This too confronts the situatedness issue.

The specific model of computation used was not originally based on biological models. It was one arrived at by continuously refining attempts to program a robot to reactively avoid collisions in a people-populated environment (Brooks 1986). Now, however, in stating the

---

[27] This constraint has slipped a little recently as we are working on building prototype small legged planetary rovers (Angle & Brooks 1990). We have built a special purpose environment for the robots—a physically simulated lunar surface.

principles used in the model of computation, it is clear that it shares certain properties with models of how neurological systems are arranged. It is important to emphasize that it only shares certain properties. Our model of computation is not intended as a realistic model of how neurological systems work. We call our computation model the *subsumption architecture* and its purpose is to program intelligent, situated, embodied agents.

Our principles of computation are:

- Computation is organized as an asynchronous network of active computational elements (they are *augmented finite state machines* — see Brooks (1989) for details[28]), with a fixed topology network of uni-directional connections.

- Messages sent over connections have no implicit semantics—they are small numbers (typically 8 or 16 bits, but on some robots just 1 bit) and their meanings are dependent on the dynamics designed into both the sender and receiver.

- Sensors and actuators are connected to this network, usually through asynchronous two-sided buffers.

These principles lead to certain consequences. In particular:

- The system can certainly have state—it is not at all constrained to be purely reactive.

- Pointers and manipulable data structures are very hard to implement (since the model is Turing equivalent it is of course possible, but hardly within the spirit).

- Any search space must be quite bounded in size, as search nodes cannot be dynamically created and destroyed during the search process.

- There is no implicit separation of data and computation, they are both distributed over the same network of elements.

In considering the biological observations outlined in section 4, certain properties seemed worth incorporating into the way in which robots are programmed within the given model of computation. In all the robots built in the mobot lab, the following principles of organization of intelligence have been observed:

---

[28] For programming convenience we use a higher level abstraction known as the *Behavior Language*, documented in Brooks (1990*a*). It compiles down to a network of machines as described above.

- There is no central model maintained of the world. All data is distributed over many computational elements.

- There is no central locus of control.

- There is no separation into perceptual system, central system, and actuation system. Pieces of the network may perform more than one of these functions. More importantly, there is intimate intertwining of aspects of all three of them.

- The behavioral competence of the system is improved by adding more behavior-specific network to the existing network. We call this process *layering*. This is a simplistic and crude analogy to evolutionary development. As with evolution, at every stage of the development the systems are tested—unlike evolution there is a gentle debugging process available. Each of the layers is a behavior-producing piece of network in its own right, although it may implicitly rely on presence of earlier pieces of network.

- There is no hierarchical arrangement—i.e., there is no notion of one process calling on another as a subroutine. Rather the networks are designed so that needed computations will simply be available on the appropriate input line when needed. There is no explicit synchronization between a producer and a consumer of messages. Message reception buffers can be overwritten by new messages before the consumer has looked at the old one. It is not atypical for a message producer to send 10 messages for every one that is examined by the receiver.

- The layers, or behaviors, all run in parallel. There may need to be a conflict resolution mechanism when different behaviors try to give different actuator commands.

- The world is often a good communication medium for processes, or behaviors, within a single robot.

It should be clear that these principles are quite different to the ones we have become accustomed to using as we program Von Neumann machines. It necessarily forces the programmer to use a different style of organization for their programs for intelligence.

There are also always influences on approaches to building thinking machines that lie outside the realm of purely logical or scientific thought. The following, perhaps arbitrary, principles have also had an influence on the organization of intelligence that has been used in Mobot Lab robots:

- A decision was made early on that all computation should be done onboard the robots. This was so that the robots could run tether-free and without any communication link. The idea is to download programs over cables (although in the case of some of our earlier robots the technique was to plug in a newly written erasable ROM) into non-volatile storage on the robots, then switch them on to interact with and be situated in the environment.

- In order to maintain a long term goal of being able to eventually produce very tiny robots (Flynn 1989) the computational model has been restricted so that any specification within that model could be rather easily compiled into a silicon circuit. This has put an additional constraint on designers of agent software, in that they cannot use non-linear numbers of connections between collections of computational elements, as that would lead to severe silicon compilation problems. Note that the general model of computation outlined above is such that a goal of silicon compilation is in general quite realistic.

The point of section 3 was to show how the technology of available computation had a major impact on the shape of the developing field of Artificial Intelligence. Likewise there have been a number of influences on my own work that are technological in nature. These include:

- Given the smallness in overall size of the robots there is a very real limitation on the amount of onboard computation that can be carried, and by an earlier principle all computation must be done onboard. The limiting factor on the amount of portable computation is not weight of the computers directly, but the electrical power that is available to run them. Empirically we have observed that the amount of electrical power available is proportional to the weight of the robot.[29]

- Since there are many single chip microprocessors available including EEPROM and RAM, it is becoming more possible to include large numbers of sensors which require interrupt servicing, local calibration, and data massaging. The microprocessors can significantly reduce the overall wiring complexity by servicing a local group of sensors (e.g., all those on a single leg of a robot) *in situ*, and packaging up the data to run over a communication network to the behavior-producing network.

---

[29] Jon Connell, a former member of the Mobot Lab, plotted data from a large number of mobile robots and noted the empirical fact that there is roughly one watt of electrical power available for onboard computation for every pound of overall weight of the robot. We call this *Connell's Law*.

These principles have been used in the programming of a number of behavior-based robots. Below we point out the importance of some of these robot demonstrations in indicating how the subsumption architecture (or one like it in spirit) can be expected to scale up to very intelligent applications. In what follows individual references are given to the most relevant piece of the literature. For a condensed description of what each of the robots is and how they are programmed, the reader should see Brooks (1990c); it also includes a number of robots not mentioned here.

6.2   Reactivity

The earliest demonstration of the subsumption architecture was on the robot *Allen* (Brooks 1986). It was almost entirely reactive, using sonar readings to keep away from people and other moving obstacles, while not colliding with static obstacles. It also had a non-reactive higher level layer that would select a goal to head towards, and then proceed to that location while the lower level reactive layer took care of avoiding obstacles.

The very first subsumption robot thus combined non-reactive capabilities with reactive ones. But the important point is that it used exactly the same sorts of computational mechanism to do both. In looking at the network of the combined layers there was no obvious partition into lower and higher level components based on the type of information flowing on the connections, or the state machines that were the computational elements. To be sure, there was a difference in function between the two layers, but there was no need to introduce any centralization or explicit representations to achieve a higher level, or later, process having useful and effective influence over a lower level.

The second robot, *Herbert* (Connell 1989), pushed on the reactive approach. It used a laser scanner to find soda can-like objects visually, infrared proximity sensors to navigate by following walls and going through doorways, a magnetic compass to maintain a global sense of orientation, and a host of sensors on an arm which were sufficient to reliably pick up soda cans. The task for Herbert was to wander around looking for soda cans, pick one up, and bring it back to where Herbert had started from. It was demonstrated reliably finding soda cans in rooms using its laser range finder (some tens of trials), picking up soda cans many times (over 100 instances), reliably navigating (many hours of runs), and in one finale doing all the tasks together to navigate, locate, pickup and return with a soda can.[30]

---

[30] The limiting factor on Herbert was the mechanical seating of its chips—its mean time between chip seating failure was no more than 15 minutes.

In programming Herbert it was decided that it should maintain no state longer than three seconds, and that there would be no internal communication between behavior generating modules. Each one was connected to sensors on the input side, and a fixed priority arbitration network on the output side. The arbitration network drove the actuators.

In order to carry out its tasks, Herbert, in many instances, had to use the world as its own best model and as a communication medium. E.g., the laser-based soda can object finder drove the robot so that its arm was lined up in front of the soda can. But it did not tell the arm controller that there was now a soda can ready to be picked up. Rather, the arm behaviors monitored the shaft encoders on the wheels, and when they noticed that there was no body motion, initiated motions of the arm, which in turn triggered other behaviors, so that eventually the robot would pick up the soda can.

The advantage of this approach is was that there was no need to set up internal expectations for what was going to happen next; that meant that the control system could both (1) be naturally opportunistic if fortuitous circumstances presented themselves, and (2) it could easily respond to changed circumstances, such as some other object approaching it on a collision course.

As one example of how the arm behaviors cascaded upon one another, consider actually grasping a soda can. The hand had a grasp reflex that operated whenever something broke an infrared beam between the fingers. When the arm located a soda can with its local sensors, it simply drove the hand so that the two fingers lined up on either side of the can. The hand then independently grasped the can. Given this arrangement, it was possible for a human to hand a soda can to the robot. As soon as it was grasped, the arm retracted—it did not matter whether it was a soda can that was intentionally grasped, or one that magically appeared. The same opportunism among behaviors let the arm adapt automatically to a wide variety of cluttered desktops, and still successfully find the soda can.

In order to return to where it came from after picking up a soda can, Herbert used a trick. The navigation routines could carry implement rules such as: *when passing through a door southbound, turn left.* These rules were conditionalized on the separation of the fingers on the hand. When the robot was outbound with no can in its hand, it effectively executed one set of rules. After picking up a can, it would execute a different set. By carefully designing the rules, Herbert was guaranteed, with reasonable reliability, to retrace its path.

The point of Herbert is two-fold.

- It demonstrates complex, apparently goal directed and intentional, behavior in a system which has no long term internal state and no internal communication.

- It is very easy for an observer of a system to attribute more complex internal structure than really exists. Herbert appeared to be doing things like path planning and map building, even though it was not.

6.3   Representation

My earlier paper Brooks (1991c) is often criticized for advocating absolutely no representation of the world within a behavior-based robot. This criticism is invalid. I make it clear in the paper that I reject traditional Artificial Intelligence representation schemes (see section 5). I also made it clear that I reject explicit representations of goals within the machine.

There can, however, be representations which are partial models of the world—in fact I mentioned that "individual layers extract only those *aspects* of the world which they find relevant—projections of a representation into a simple subspace" (Brooks 1991c). The form these representations take, within the context of the computational model we are using, will depend on the particular task those representations are to be used for. For more general navigation than that demonstrated by Connell it may sometimes[31] need to build and maintain a map.

Mataric (1990c) and Mataric (1991) introduced *active-constructive representations* to subsumption in a sonar-based robot, *Toto*, which wandered around office environments building a map based on landmarks, and then used that map to get from one location to another. Her representations were totally decentralized and non-manipulable, and there is certainly no central control which build, maintains, or uses the maps. Rather, the map itself is an active structure which does the computations necessary for any path planning the robot needs to do.

Primitive layers of control let Toto wander around following boundaries (such as walls and furniture clutter) in an indoor environment. A layer which detects landmarks, such as flat clear walls, corridors, etc., runs in parallel. It informs the map layer as its detection certainty exceeds a fixed threshold. The map is represented as a graph internally. The nodes of the graph are computational elements (they are identical little subnetworks of distinct augmented finite state machines). Free

---

[31] Note that we are saying only *sometimes*, not *must*—there are many navigation tasks doable by mobile robots which appear intelligent, but which do not require map information at all.

nodes arbitrate and allocate themselves, in a purely local fashion, to represent a new landmark, and set up topological links to physically neighboring nodes (using a limited capacity switching network to keep the total virtual 'wire length' between finite state machines to be linear in the map capacity). These nodes keep track of where the robot is physically, by observing changes in the output of the landmark detector, and comparing that to predictions they have made by local message passing, and by referring to other more primitive (magnetic compass based) coarse position estimation schemes.

When a higher layer wants the robot to go to some known landmark, it merely 'excites', in some particular way the particular place in the map that it wants to go. The excitation (this is an abstraction programmed into the particular finite state machines used here—it is not a primitive—as such there could be many different types of excitation co-existing in the map, if other types of planning are required) is spread through the map following topological links, estimating total path link, and arriving at the *landmark-that-I'm-at-now* node (a deictic representation) with a recommendation of the direction to travel right now to follow the shortest path. As the robot moves so to does its representation of where it is, and at that new node the arriving excitation tells it where to go next. The map thus bears a similarity to the *internalized plans* of Payton (1990), but it represented by the same computational elements that use it—there is no distinction between data and process. Furthermore Mataric's scheme can have multiple simultaneously active goals—the robot will simply head towards the nearest one.

This work demonstrates the following aspects of behavior-based or subsumption systems:

- Such systems can make predictions about what will happen in the world, and have expectations.

- Such systems can make plans—but they are not the same as traditional Artificial Intelligence plans—see Agre & Chapman (1990) for an analysis of this issue.

- Such systems can have goals—see Maes (1990a) for another way to implement goals within the approach.

- All these things can be done without resorting to central representations.

- All these things can be done without resorting to manipulable representations.

- All these things can be done without resorting to symbolic representations.

6.4   Complexity

Can subsumption-like approaches scale to arbitrarily complex systems? This is a question that cannot be answered affirmatively right now—just as it is totally unfounded to answer the same question affirmatively in the case of traditional symbolic Artificial Intelligence methods. The best one can do is point to precedents and trends.

There are a number of dimensions along which the scaling question can be asked. E.g.,

- Can the approach work well as the environment becomes more complex?

- Can the approach handle larger numbers of sensors and actuators?

- Can the approach work smoothly as more and more layers or behaviors are added?

We answer each of these in turn in the following paragraphs.

The approach taken at the Mobot Lab has been that from day one always test the robot in the most complex environment for which it is ultimately destined. This forces even the simplest levels to handle the most complex environment expected. So for a given robot and intended environment the scaling question is handled by the methodology chosen for implementation. But there is also the question of how complex are the environments that are targeted for with the current generation of robots. Almost all of our robots have been tested and operated in indoor environments with people unrelated to the research wandering through their work area at will. Thus we have a certain degree of confidence that the same basic approach will work in outdoor environments (the sensory processing will have to change for some sensors) with other forms of dynamic action taking place.

The number of sensors and actuators possessed by today's robots are pitiful when compared to the numbers in even simple organisms such as insects. Our first robots had only a handful of identical sonar sensors and two motors. Later a six legged walking robot was built (Angle 1989b). It had 12 actuators and 20 sensors, and was successfully programmed in subsumption (Brooks 1989) to walk adaptively over rough terrain. The key was to find the right factoring into sensor and actuator subsystems so that interactions between the subsystems could be minimized. A new six legged robot, recently completed (Angle & Brooks 1990), is much more challenging, but still nowhere near the complexity of insects. It has 23 actuators and over 150 sensors. With this level of sensing it is possible to start to develop some of the 'senses' that animals and humans have, such as a kinesthetic sense—this comes from the contributions of many sensor readings. Rather, than feed into a geometric model the sensors feed into a estimate of bodily motion. There is also the question of the types of sensors used. Horswill & Brooks (1988) generalized the subsumption architecture so that some of the connections between processing elements could be a *retina bus*, a cable that transmitted partially processed images from one site to another within the system. The robot so programmed was able to follow corridors and follow moving objects in real time.

As we add more layers we find that the interactions can become more complex. Maes (1989) introduced the notion of switching whole pieces of the network on and off, using an *activation* scheme for behaviors. That idea is now incorporated into the subsumption methodology (Brooks 1990a), and provides a way of implementing both competition and cooperation between behaviors. At a lower level a hormone-like system has been introduced (Brooks 1991a) which models the hormone system of the lobster (Kravitz 1988) (Arkin (1989) had implemented a system with similar inspiration). With these additional control mechanisms we have certainly bought ourselves breathing room to increase the performance of our systems markedly. The key point about these control systems is that they fit exactly into the existing structures, and are totally distributed and local in their operations.

6.5 Learning

Evolution has decided that there is a tradeoff between what we know through our genes and what we must find out for ourselves as we develop. We can expect to see a similar tradeoff for our behavior-based robots.

There are at least four classes of things that can be learned:

1. representations of the world that help in some task

2. aspects of instances of sensors and actuators (this is sometimes called calibration)

3. the ways in which individual behaviors should interact

4. new behavioral modules

The robots in the Mobot Lab have been programmed to demonstrate the first three of these types of learning. The last one has not yet been successfully tackled.[32]

Learning representations of the world was already discussed above concerning the work of Mataric (1990c) and Mataric (1991). The next

---

[32] We did have a failed attempt at this through simulated evolution—this is the approach taken by many in the Artificial Life movement.

step will be to generalize active-constructive representations to more classes of use.

Viola (1990) demonstrated calibration of a complex head-eye system modeling the primate vestibulo-ocular system. In this system there is one fast channel between a gyroscope and a high performance pan-tilt head holding the camera, and a slower channel using vision which produces correction signals for the gyroscope channel. The same system was used to learn how to accurately saccade to moving stimuli.

Lastly, Maes & Brooks (1990) programmed an early six legged robot to learn to walk using the subsumption architecture along with the behavior activation schemes of Maes (1989). Independent behaviors on each leg monitored the activity of other behaviors and correlated that, their own activity state, and the results from a belly switch which provided negative feedback, as input to a local learning rule which learned under which conditions it was to operate the behavior. After about 20 trials per leg, spread over a total of a minute or two, the robot reliably learns the alternating tripod gait—it slowly seems to emerge out of initially chaotic flailing of the legs.

Learning within subsumption is in its early stages but it has been demonstrated in a number of different critical modes of development.

6.6   Vistas

The behavior-based approach has been demonstrated on situated embodied systems doing things that traditional Artificial Intelligence would have tackled in quite different ways. What are the key research areas that need to be addressed in order to push behavior-based robots towards more and more sophisticated capabilities?

In this section we outline research challenges in three categories or levels:[33]

- Understanding the dynamics of how an individual behavior couples with the environment via the robot's sensors and actuators. The primary concerns here are what forms of perception are necessary, and what relationships exist between perception, internal state, and action (i.e., how behavior is specified or described).

- Understanding how many behaviors can be integrated into a single robot. The primary concerns here are how independent various perceptions and behaviors can be, how much they must rely on, and interfere with each other, how a competent complete robot can

---

[33] The reader is referred to Brooks (1990b) for a more complete discussion of these issues.

be built in such a way as to accommodate all the required individual behaviors, and to what extent apparently complex behaviors can emerge from simple reflexes.

- Understanding how multiple robots (either a homogeneous, or a heterogeneous group) can interact as they go about their business. The primary concerns here are the relationships between individuals' behaviors, the amount and type of communication between robots, the way the environment reacts to multiple individuals, and the resulting patterns of behavior and their impacts upon the environment (which night not occur in the case of isolated individuals).

Just as research in Artificial Intelligence is broken into subfields, these categories provide subfields of behavior-based robots within which it is possible to concentrate a particular research project. Some of these topics are theoretical in nature, contributing to a science of behavior-based systems. Others are engineering in nature, providing tools and mechanisms for successfully building and programming behavior-based robots. Some of these topics have already been touched upon by researchers in behavior-based approaches, but none of them are yet solved or completely understood.

At the individual behavior level some of the important issues are as follows:

Convergence: Demonstrate or prove that a specified behavior is such that the robot will indeed carry out the desired task successfully. For instance, we may want to give some set of initial conditions for a robot, and some limitations on possible worlds in which it is placed, and show that under those conditions, the robot is guaranteed to follow a particular wall, rather than diverge and get lost.

Synthesis: Given a particular task, automatically derive a behavior specification for the creature so that it carries out that task in a way which has clearly demonstrable convergence. I do not expect progress in this topic in the near future.

Complexity: Deal with the complexity of real world environments, and sift out the relevant aspects of received sensations rather than being overwhelmed with a multitude of data.

Learning: Develop methods for the automatic acquisition of new behaviors, and the modification and tuning of existing behaviors.

As multiple behaviors are built into a single robot the following issues need to be addressed:

Coherence: Even though many behaviors may be active at once, or are being actively switched on or off, the robot should still appear to an observer to have coherence of action and goals. It should not be rapidly switching between inconsistent behaviors, nor should two behaviors be active simultaneously, if they interfere with each other to the point that neither operates successfully.

Relevance: The behaviors that are active should be relevant to the situation the robot finds itself in—e.g., it should recharge itself when the batteries are low, not when they are full.

Adequacy: The behavior selection mechanism must operate in such a way that the long term goals that the robot designer has for the robot are met—e.g., a floor cleaning robot should successfully clean the floor in normal circumstances, besides doing all the ancillary tasks that are necessary for it to be successful at that.

Representation: Multiple behaviors might want to share partial representations of the world—in fact the representations of world aspects might generate multiple behaviors when activated appropriately.

Learning: The performance of a robot might be improved by adapting the ways in which behaviors interact, or are activated, as a result of experience.

When many behavior-based robots start to interact there are a whole new host of issues which arise. Many of these same issues would arise if the robots were built using traditional Artificial Intelligence methods, but there has been very little published in these areas.

Emergence: Given a set of behaviors programmed into a set of robots, we would like to be able to predict what the global behavior of the system will be, and as a consequence determine the differential effects of small changes to the individual robots on the global behavior.

Synthesis: As at single behavior level, given a particular task, automatically derive a program for the set of robots so that they carry out the task.

Communication: Performance may be increased by increasing the amount of explicit communication between robots, but the relationship between the amount of communication increase and performance increase needs to be understood.

Cooperation: In some circumstances robots should be able to achieve more by cooperating—the form and specification of such possible cooperations need to be understood.

Interference: Robots may interfere with one another. Protocols for avoiding this when it is undesirable must be included in the design of the creatures' instructions.

Density dependence: The global behavior of the system may be dependent on the density of the creatures and the resources they consume within the world. A characterization of this dependence is desirable. At the two ends of the spectrum it may be the case that (a) a single robot given n units of time performs identically to n robots each given 1 unit of time, and (2) the global task might not be achieved at all if there are fewer than, say, m robots.

Individuality: Robustness can be achieved if all robots are interchangeable. A fixed number of classes of robots, where all robots within a class are identical, is also robust, but somewhat less so. The issue then is to, given a task, decide how many classes of creatures are necessary

Learning: The performance of the robots may increase in two ways through learning. At one level, when one robot learns some skill if might be able to transfer it to another. At another level, the robots might learn cooperative strategies.

These are a first cut at topics of interest within behavior-based approaches. As we explore more we will find more topics, and some that seem interesting now will turn out to be irrelevant.

6.7 Thinking

Can this approach lead to thought? How could it? It seems the antithesis of thought. But we must ask first, what is thought? Like intelligence this is a very slippery concept.

We only know that thought exists in biological systems through our own introspection. At one level we identify thought with the product of our consciousness, but that too is a contentious subject, and one which has had little attention from Artificial Intelligence.

My feeling is that thought and consciousness are epi-phenomena of the process of being in the world. As the complexity of the world increases, and the complexity of processing to deal with that world rises, we will see the same evidence of thought and consciousness in our systems as we see in people other than ourselves now. Thought and consciousness will not need to be programmed in. They will emerge.

7 Conclusion

The title of this paper is intentionally ambiguous. The following interpretations all encapsulate important points.

- An earlier paper Brooks (1991c)[34] was titled *Intelligence without Representation*. The thesis of that paper was that intelligent behavior could be generated without having explicit manipulable internal representations. *Intelligence without Reason* is thus complementary, stating that intelligent behavior can be generated without having explicit reasoning systems present.

- *Intelligence without Reason* can be read as a statement that intelligence is an emergent property of certain complex systems—it sometimes arises without an easily identifiable reason for arising.

- *Intelligence without Reason* can be viewed as a commentary on the bandwagon effect in research in general, and in particular in the case of Artificial Intelligence research. Many lines of research have become goals of pursuit in their own right, with little recall of the reasons for pursuing those lines. A little grounding occasionally can go a long way towards helping keep things on track.

- *Intelligence without Reason* is also a commentary on the way evolution built intelligence—rather than reason about how to build intelligent systems, it used a generate and test strategy. This is in stark contrast to the way all human endeavors to build intelligent systems must inevitably proceed. Furthermore we must be careful in emulating the results of evolution—there may be many structures and observable properties which are suboptimal or vestigial.

We are a long way from creating Artificial Intelligences that measure up the to the standards of early ambitions for the field. It is a complex endeavor and we sometimes need to step back and question why we are proceeding in the direction we are going, and look around for other promising directions.

---

[34] Despite the publication date it was written in 1986 and 1987, and was complete in its published form in 1987.

Acknowledgements

Maja Mataric reviewed numerous drafts of this paper and gave helpful criticism at every stage of the process. Lynne Parker, Anita Flynn, Ian Horswill and Pattie Maes gave me much constructive feedback on later drafts.

Support for this research was provided in part by the University Research Initiative under Office of Naval Research contract N00014–86–K–0685, in part by the Advanced Research Projects Agency under Office of Naval Research contrat N00014–85–K–0124, in part by the Hughes Artificial Intelligence Center, in part by Siemens Corporation, and in part by Mazda Corporation.

Bibliography

Agre, P. E. (1988), The Dynamic Structure of Everyday Life, Technical Report 1085, Massachusetts Institute of Technology Artificial Intelligence Lab, Cambridge, Massachusetts.

Agre, P. E. (1991), *The Dynamic Structure of Everyday Life*, Cambridge University Press, Cambridge, United Kingdom.

Agre, P. E. & Chapman, D. (1987), "Pengi: An Implementation of a Theory of Activity", in *Proceedings of the Sixth Annual Meeting of the American Association for Artificial Intelligence*, Morgan Kaufmann Publishers, Seattle, Washington, pp. 268–272. Also appeared in Luger (1995).

Agre, P. E. & Chapman, D. (1990), "What Are Plans For?", *Robotics and Autonomous Systems* 6(1,2), 17–34. Also appeared in Maes (1990b).

Agre, P. E. & Chapman, D. (n.d.), "Unpublished memo", MIT Artificial Intelligence Lab. Cambridge, Massachusetts.

Angle, C. M. (1989a), "Atilla's Crippled Brother Marvin", MIT Term Paper in Electrical Engineering and Computer Science.

Angle, C. M. (1989b), Genghis, a Six Legged Walking Robot, Master's thesis, Massachusetts Institute of Technology, Cambridge, Massachusetts. Bachelor's thesis.

Angle, C. M. & Brooks, R. A. (1990), "Small Planetary Rovers", in *IEEE/RSJ International Workshop on Intelligent Robots and Systems*, Ikabara, Japan, pp. 383–388.

Arbib, M. A. (1964), *Brains, Machines and Mathematics*, McGraw-Hill, New York, New York.

Arkin, R. C. (1989), "Towards the Unification of Navigational Planning and Reactive Control", in *AAAI Spring Symposium on Robot Navigation and Working Notes*, pp. 1–5.

Arkin, R. C. (1990), "Integrating Behavioral, Perceptual and World Knowledge in Reactive Navigation", *Robotics and Autonomous Systems* 6(1,2), 105–122. Also appeared in Maes (1990b).

Ashby, W. R. (1952), *Design for a Brain*, Chapman and Hall, London, United Kingdom.

Ashby, W. R. (1956), *An Introduction to Cybernetics*, Chapman and Hall, London, United Kingdom.

Atkeson, C. G. (1989), Using Local Models to Control Movement, in D. S. Touretzky, ed., *Neural Information Processing 2*, Morgan Kaufmann Publishers, Los Altos, California, pp. 316–324.

Ballard, D. H. (1989), "Reference Frames for Animate Vision", in *Proceedings of the Eleventh International Joint Conference on Artificial Intelligence*, Morgan Kaufmann Publishers, Detroit, Michigan, pp. 1635–1641.

Barrow, H. & Salter, S. (1970), Design of Low-Cost Equipment for Cognitive Robot Research, in B. Meltzer & D. Michie, eds, *Machine Intelligence 5*, American Elsevier Publishing, New York, New York, pp. 555–566.

Bassler, U. (1983), *Neural Basis of Elementary Behavior in Stick Insects*, Springer-Verlag.

Beer, R. D. (1990), *Intelligence as Adaptive Behavior*, Academic Press, San Diego, California.

Bergland, R. (1985), *The Fabric of Mind*, Viking, New York, New York.

Bizzi, E. (1980), Central and peripheral mechanisms in motor control, in G. Stelmach & J. Requin, eds, *Tutorials in Motor Behavior*, North-Holland.

Bloom, F. (1976), "Endorphins: Profound Behavioral Effects", *Science* **194**, 630–634.

Bobrow, R. J. & Brown, J. S. (1975), Systematic Understanding: Synthesis, Analysis, and Contingent Knowledge in Specialized Understanding Systems, in Bobrow & Collins, eds, *Representation and Understanding*, Academic Press, New York, New York, pp. 103–129.

Brachman, R. J. & Levesque, H. J. (1985), *Readings in Knowledge Representation*, Morgan Kaufmann Publishers, Los Altos, California.

Brady, D. (1990), "Switching Arrays Make Light Work in a Simple Processor", *Nature* **344**, 486–487.

Brady, M., Hollerbach, J., Johnson, T. & Lozano-Pérez, T., eds (1982), *Robot Motion: Planning and Control*, MIT Press, Cambridge, Massachusetts.

Braitenberg, V. (1984), *Vehicles: Experiments in Synthetic Psychology*, MIT Press, Cambridge, Massachusetts.

Brooks, R. A. (1981), "Symbolic Reasoning Among 3-D Models and 2-D Images", *Artificial Intelligence Journal* **17**, 285–348.

Brooks, R. A. (1982), "Symbolic Error Analysis and Robot Planning", *International Journal of Robotics Research* **1**(4), 29–68.

Brooks, R. A. (1984a), Aspects of mobile robot visual map making, in Hanafusa & Inoue, eds, *Robotics Research 2*, MIT, Cambridge, Massachusetts, pp. 369–375.

Brooks, R. A. (1984b), *Model-Based Computer Vision*, UMI Research Press, Ann Arbor, Michigan.

Brooks, R. A. (1985), "Visual Map Making for a Mobile Robot", in *Proceedings of the 1985 IEEE Conference on Robotics and Automation*, pp. 824–829.

Brooks, R. A. (1986), "A Robust Layered Control System for a Mobile Robot", *IEEE Journal of Robotics and Automation* **RA-2**, 14–23.

Brooks, R. A. (1987), "Micro-Brains for Micro-Brawn: Autonomous Micro-robots", in *IEEE Micro Robots and Teleoperators Workshop*, Hyannis, Massachusetts.

Brooks, R. A. (1989), "A Robot That Walks: Emergent Behavior from a Carefully Evolved Network", *Neural Computation* **1**(2), 253–262.

Brooks, R. A. (1990*a*), The Behavior Language User's Guide, Memo 1227, Massachusetts Institute of Technology Artificial Intelligence Lab, Cambridge, Massachusetts.

Brooks, R. A. (1990*b*), "Challenges for Complete Creature Architectures", in *Proceedings of the First International Conference on Simulation of Adaptive Behavior*, MIT Press, Cambridge, Massachusetts, pp. 434–443.

Brooks, R. A. (1990*c*), "Elephants Don't Play Chess", *Robotics and Autonomous Systems* **6**(1,2), 3–15. Also appeared in Maes (1990*b*).

Brooks, R. A. (1991*a*), "Integrated Systems Based on Behaviors", *SIGART, Special Issue on Integrated Intelligent Systems*.

Brooks, R. A. (1991*b*), "Intelligence Without Reason", in *Proceedings of the 1991 International Joint Conference on Artificial Intelligence*, pp. 569–595. Also appeared in Steels & Brooks (1995).

Brooks, R. A. (1991*c*), "Intelligence Without Representation", *Artificial Intelligence Journal* **47**, 139–160. Also appeared in Luger (1995).

Brooks, R. A. & Connell, J. (1986), "Asynchronous Distributed Control System for a Mobile Robot", in *SPIE's Cambridge Symposium on Optical and Opto-Electronic Engineering Proceedings, Vol. 727*, pp. 77–84.

Brooks, R. A. & Flynn, A. M. (1989), "Robot Beings", in *IEEE/RSJ International Workshop on Intelligent Robots and Systems*, Tsukuba, Japan, pp. 2–10.

Brooks, R. A., Connell, J. H. & Ning, P. (1988), Herbert: A Second Generation Mobile Robot, Memo 1016, Massachusetts Institute of Technology Artificial Intelligence Lab, Cambridge, Massachusetts.

Brooks, R. A., Flynn, A. M. & Marill, T. (1987), Self Calibration of Motion and Stereo for Mobile Robot Navigation, Memo 984, Massachusetts Institute of Technology Artificial Intelligence Lab, Cambridge, Massachusetts.

Campbell, J. (1983), Go, in M. Bramer, ed., *Computer Game-Playing: Theory and Practice*, Ellis Horwood, Chichester, United Kingdom.

Chapman, D. (1987), "Planning for Conjunctive Goals", *Artificial Intelligence Journal* **32**, 333–377.

Chapman, D. (1990), Vision, Instruction and Action, Technical Report 1085, Massachusetts Institute of Technology Artificial Intelligence Lab, Cambridge, Massachusetts.

Charniak, E. & McDermott, D. (1984), *Introduction to Artificial Intelligence*, Addison-Wesley, Reading, Massachusettse.

Chatila, R. & Laumond, J. (1985), "Position Referencing and Consistent World Modeling for Mobile Robots", in *IEEE International Conference on Robotics and Automation*, pp. 138–145.

Churchland, P. S. (1986), *Neurophilosophy: Toward a Unified Science of the Mind/Brain*, MIT Press, Cambridge, Massachusetts.

Cohen, L. & Wu, J.-Y. (1990), "One Neuron, Many Units?", *Nature* **346**, 108–109.

Cohen, P. R. (1991), "A Survey of the Eigth National Conference on Artificial Intelligence: Pulling Together or Pulling APart?", *AI Magazine*.

Condon, J. & Thompson, K. (1984), Belle, in P. Frey, ed., *Chess Skill in Man and Machine*, Springer-Verlag.

Connell, J. H. (1987), "Creature Building with the Subsumption Architecture", in *Proceedings of the International Joint Conference on Artificial Intelligence*, Milan, Italy, pp. 1124–1126.

Connell, J. H. (1988), A Behavior-Based Arm Controller, Memo 1025, Massachusetts Institute of Technology Artificial Intelligence Lab, Cambridge, Massachusetts.

Connell, J. H. (1989), A Colony Architecture for an Artificial Creature, Technical Report 1151, Massachusetts Institute of Technology Artificial Intelligence Lab, Cambridge, Massachusetts.

Cox, I. & Wilfong, G., eds (1990), *Autonomous Robot Vehicles*, Springer Verlag, New York, New York.

Crowley, J. I. (1985), "Navigation for an intelligent mobile robot", *IEEE Journal of Robotics and Automation* **RA-1**(1), 31–41.

Cruse, H. (1990), "What Mechanisms Coordinate Leg Movement in Walking Arthropods?", *Trends in Neurosciences* **13**(1), 15–21.

de Kleer, J. & Brown, J. S. (1984), "A Qualitative Physics Based on Confluences", *Artificial Intelligence Journal* **24**, 7–83.

Dennett, D. C. & Kinsbourne, M. (1990), Time and the Observer: the Where and When of Consciousness in the Brain, Technical report, Center for Cognitive Studies, Tufts University.

Dickmanns, E. D. & Graefe, V. (1988), "Dynamic Monocular Machine Vision", *Machine Vision and Applications* **1**, 223–240.

Dreyfus, H. L. (1981), From Micro-Worlds to Knowledge Representation: AI at an Impasse, in J. Haugeland, ed., *Mind Design*, MIT Press, Cambridge, Massachusetts, pp. 161–204.

Drumheller, M. (1985), Robot Localization Using Range Data, Master's thesis, MIT Dept. of Mechanical Engineering, Cambridge, Massachusetts. Bachelor's thesis.

Eichenbaum, H., Wiener, S., Shapiro, M. & Cohen, N. (1989), "The organization of spatial coding in the hippocampus: A study of neural ensemble activity", *Journal of Neuroscience* **9**(8), 2764–2775.

Elfes, A. & Talukdar, S. (1983), "A distributed control system for the CMU rover", in *Proceedings IJCAI-83*, pp. 830–833.

Ernst, H. A. (1961), A Computer-Operated Mechanical Hand, PhD thesis, Massachusetts Institute of Technology, Cambridge, Massachusetts.

Evans, T. G. (1968), A Program for the Solution of Geometric-Analogy Intelligence Test Questions, in M. Minsky, ed., *Semantic Information Processing*, MIT Press, Cambridge, Massachusetts, pp. 271–353.

Fahlman, S. E. (1974), "A Planning System for Robot Construction", *Artificial Intelligence Journal* **5**, 1–50.

Feigenbaum, E. A. & Feldman, J. (1963), *Computers and Thought*, McGraw-Hill, New York, New York.

Firby, R. J. (1989), Adaptive Execution in Dynamic Domains, PhD thesis, Yale University.

Flynn, A. M. (1985), Redundant sensors for mobile robot navigation, Master's thesis, MIT, Cambridge, Massachusetts.

Flynn, A. M. (1988), "Gnat Robots: A Low-Intelligence, Low-Cost Approach", in *IEEE Solid-State Sensor and Actuator Workshop*, Hilton Head, South Carolina.

Flynn, A. M. (1989), "Gnat Robots (And How They Will Change Robotics)", in *IEEE Micro Robots and Teleoperators Workshop*, Hyannis, Massachusetts.

Flynn, A. M., Brooks, R. A. & Tavrow, L. S. (1989*a*), Twilight Zones and Cornerstones: A Gnat Robot Double Feature, Memo 1126, Massachusetts Institute of Technology Artificial Intelligence Lab, Cambridge, Massachusetts.

Flynn, A. M., Brooks, R. A., Wells, W. M. & Barrett, D. S. (1989*b*), "The World's Largest One Cubic Inch Robot", in *Proceedings IEEE Micro Electro Mechanical Systems*, Salt Lake City, Utah, pp. 98–101.

Gazzaniga, M. S. & LeDoux, J. E. (1977), *The Integrated Mind*, Plenum, New York, New York.

Gibbs, H. (1985), *Optical Bistability: Controlling Light with Light*, Academic Press, New York, New York.

Giralt, G., Chatila, R. & Vaisset, M. (1984), An Integrated Navigation and Motion Control System for Autonomous Multisensory Robots, in Brady & Paul, eds, *Robotics Research 1*, MIT Press, Cambridge, Massachusetts, pp. 191–214. Also appeared in Cox & Wilfong (1990).

Götz, K. G. & Wenking, H. (1973), "Visual Control of Locomotion in the Walking Fruitfly *Drosophila*", *Journal of Comparative Physiology* **85**, 235–266.

Gould, J. L. & Marler, P. (1986), "Learning by Instinct", *Scientific American* pp. 74–85.

Gould, S. & Eldredge, N. (1977), "Punctuated Equilibria: The Tempo and Mode of Evolution Reconsidered", *Paleobiology* **3**, 115–151.

Greenblatt, R., Eastlake, D. & Crocker, S. (1967), "The Greenblatt Chess Program", in *Am. Fed. Inf. Proc. Soc. Conference Proceedings*, pp. 801–810.

Grimson, W. E. L. (1985), "Computational experiments with a feature based stereo algorithm", *IEEE Trans. PAMI* **PAMI-7**, 17–34.

Grimson, W. E. L. (1990), *Object Recognition by Computer: The Role of Geometric Constraints*, MIT Press, Cambridge, Massachusetts.

Hartmanis, J. (1971), "Computational Complexity of Random Access Stored Program Machines", *Mathematical Systems Theory* **5**(3), 232–245.

Hayes, P. J. (1985), The Second Naive Physics Manifesto, in J. R. Hobbs & R. C. Moore, eds, *Formal Theories of the Commonsense World*, Ablex, Norwood, New Jersey, pp. 1–36. Also appeared in Luger (1995).

Hillis, W. D. (1985), *The Connection Machine*, MIT Press, Cambridge, Massachusetts.

Hodges, A. (1983), *Alan Turing: The Enigma*, Simon and Shuster, New York, New York.

Hofstadter, D. R. & Dennett, D. C. (1981), *The Mind's I*, Bantam Books, New York, New York.

Horswill, I. D. & Brooks, R. A. (1988), "Situated Vision in a Dynamic World: Chasing Objects", in *Proceedings of the Seventh Annual Meeting of the American Association for Artificial Intelligence*, St. Paul, Minnesota, pp. 796–800.

Hsu, F.-H., Anantharaman, T., Campbell, M. & Nowatzyk, A. (1990), "A Grandmaster Chess Machine", *Scientific American* **263**(4), 44–50.

Johnson, M. (1987), *The Body in the Mind: The Bodily Basis of Meaning, Imagination, and Reason*, The University of Chicago Press, Chicago, Illinois.

Kaelbling, L. P. (1990), Learning in Embedded Systems, PhD thesis, Stanford University.

Kaelbling, L. P. & Rosenschein, S. J. (1990), "Action and Planning in Embedded Agents", *Robotics and Autonomous Systems* **6**(1,2), 35–48. Also appeared in Maes (1990*b*).

Kanayama, Y. (1983), "Concurrent programming of intelligent robots", in *Proceedings of IJCAI-83*, pp. 834–838.

Khatib, O. (1983), "Dynamic control of manipulators in operational space", in *Sixth IFTOMM Cong. Theory of Machines and Mechanisms*.

Klein, C., Olson, K. & Pugh, D. (1983), "Use of force and attitude sensors for locomotion of a legged vehicle", *International Journal of Robotics Research* **2**(2), 3–17.

Knuth, D. E. & Moore, R. E. (1975), "An Analysis of Alpha-Beta Pruning", *Artificial Intelligence Journal* **6**, 293–326.

Kravitz, E. A. (1988), "Hormonal Control of Behavior: Amines and the Biasing Behavioral Output in Lobsters", *Science* **241**, 1775–1781.

Kreithen, M. (1983), Orientational strategies in birds: a tribute to W.T. Keeton, in *Behavioral Energetics: The Cost of Survival in Vertebrates*, Ohio State University, Columbus, Ohio, pp. 3–28.

Kuhn, T. S. (1970), *The Structure of Scientific Revolutions*, second, enlarged edn, The University of Chicago Press, Chicago, Illinois.

Kuipers, B. (1987), "A Qualitative Approach To Robot Exploration and Map Learning", in *AAAI Workshop on Spatial Reasoning and Multi-Sensor Fusion*.

Lenat, D. B. & Feigenbaum, E. A. (1991), "On the Thresholds of Knowledge", *Artificial Intelligence Journal* **47**, 185–250.

Lewis, A. C. (1986), "Memory Constraints and Flower Choice in Pieris Rapae", *Science* **232**, 863–865.

Lozano-Pérez, T. & Brooks, R. A. (1984), An Approach to Automatic Robot Programming, in M. S. Pickett & J. W. Boyse, eds, *Solid Modeling by Computers*, Plenum Press, New York, New York, pp. 293–328.

Lozano-Pérez, T., Jones, J. L., Mazer, E. & O'Donnell, P. A. (1989), "Task-Level Planning of Pick-and-Place Robot Motions", *IEEE Computer* **22**(3), 21–29.

Lozano-Pérez, T., Mason, M. W. & Taylor, R. H. (1984), "Automatic Synthesis of Fine-Motion Strategies for Robots", *International Journal of Robotics Research* **3**(1), 3–24.

Luger, G. F., ed. (1995), *Computation & Intelligence: Collected Readings*, AAAI Press, MIT Press, Menlo Park, California.

Maes, P. (1989), "The Dynamics of Action Selection", in *Proceedings of the Eleventh International Joint Conference on Artificial Intelligence*, Morgan Kaufmann Publishers, Detroit, Michigan, pp. 991–997.

Maes, P. (1990a), "Situated Agents Can Have Goals", *Robotics and Autonomous Systems* **6**(1,2), 49–70. Also appeared in Maes (1990b) and in the special issue of the Journal of Robotics and Autonomous Systems, Spring '90, North Holland.

Maes, P. & Brooks, R. A. (1990), "Learning to Coordinate Behaviors", in *Proceedings of the Eighth Annual Meeting of the American Association for Artificial Intelligence*, MIT Press, Cambridge, Massachusetts, pp. 796–802.

Maes, P., ed. (1990*b*), *Designing Autonomous Agents: Theory and Practice from Biology to Engineering and Back*, MIT Press, Cambridge, Massachusetts.

Mahadevan, S. & Connell, J. (1990), Automatic Programming of Behavior-Based Robots Using Reinforcement Learning, Technical report, IBM T.J. Watson Research Report.

Malcolm, C. & Smithers, T. (1990), "Symbol Grounding Via a Hybrid Architecture in an Autonomous Assembly System", *Robotics and Autonomous Systems* **6**(1,2), 123–144. Also appeared in Maes (1990*b*).

Malkin, P. K. & Addanki, S. (1990), "LOGnets: A Hybrid Graph Spatial Representation for Robot Navigation", in *Proceedings of the Eighth National Conference on Artificial Intelligence (AAAI-90)*, MIT Press, Cambridge, Massachusetts, pp. 1045–1050.

Marr, D. (1982), *Vision*, W.H. Freeman, San Francisco, California.

Mataric, M. J. (1989), "Qualitative Sonar Based Environment Learning for Mobile Robots", in *SPIE 1989 Mobile Robots IV Proceedings*.

Mataric, M. J. (1990*a*), A Distributed Model for Mobile Robot Environment-Learning and Navigation, Technical Report 1228, Massachusetts Institute of Technology Artificial Intelligence Lab, Cambridge, Massachusetts.

Mataric, M. J. (1990*b*), "Environment Learning Using a Distributed Representation", in *Proceedings of the 1990 IEEE International Conference on Robotics and Automation*, pp. 402–406.

Mataric, M. J. (1990*c*), "Navigation with a Rat Brain: A Neurobiologically-Inspired Model for Robot Spatial Representation", in *Proceedings of the First International Conference on Simulation of Adaptive Behavior*, MIT Press, Cambridge, Massachusetts, pp. 169–175.

Mataric, M. J. (1991), "Behavioral Synergy Without Explicit Integration", *SIGART, Special Issue on Integrated Intelligent Systems*.

McCarthy, J. (1960), "Recursive Functions of Symbolic Expressions", *Communications of the Association for Computing Machinery* **3**, 184–195.

McCarthy, R. A. & Warrington, E. K. (1988), "Evidence for Modality-Specific Systems in the Brain", *Nature* **334**, 428–430.

McCorduck, P. (1979), *Machines Who Think*, Freeman, New York, New York.

McCulloch, W. & Pitts, W. (1943), "A Logical Calculus of the Ideas Immanent in Nervous Activity", *Bulletin of Mathematical Biophysics* **5**, 115–137.

McDermott, D. (1987). Position paper for DARPA Santa Cruz panel on interleaving planning and execution.

McFarland, D. (1985), *Animal Behaviour*, Benjamin/Cummings, Menlo Park, California.

McFarland, D. (1988), *Problems of Animal Behaviour*, Longman, Harlow, United Kingdom.

Michie, D. & Ross, R. (1970), Experiments with the Adaptive Graph Traverser, in B. Meltzer & D. Michie, eds, *Machine Intelligence 5*, American Elsevier Publishing, New York, New York, pp. 301–318.

Minsky, M. (1954), Neural Nets and the Brain Model Problem, PhD thesis, Princeton University, Univeristy Microfilms, Ann Arbor, Michigan. Unpublished Ph.D. dissertation.

Minsky, M. (1961), "Steps Toward Artificial Intelligence", *Proceedings IRE* **49**, 8–30. Also appeared in Feigenbaum & Feldman (1963) and Luger (1995).

Minsky, M. (1963), A Selected Descriptor-Indexed Bibliography to the Literature of Artificial Intelligence, in E. A. Feigenbaum & J. Feldman, eds, *Computers and Thought*, McGraw-Hill, New York, New York, pp. 453–523.

Minsky, M. (1986), *The Society of Mind*, Simon and Schuster, New York, New York.

Minsky, M. & Papert, S. (1969), *Perceptrons*, MIT Press, Cambridge, Massachusetts.

Minsky, M., ed. (1968), *Semantic Information Processing*, MIT Press, Cambridge, Massachusetts.

Mitchell, T. M. (1990), "Becoming Increasingly Reactive", in *Proceedings of the Eighth Annual Meeting of the American Association for Artificial Intelligence*, MIT Press, Cambridge, Massachusetts, pp. 1051–1058.

Moravec, H. P. (1981), *Robot Rover Visual Navigation*, UMI Research Press, Ann Arbor, Michigan.

Moravec, H. P. (1983), "The Stanford Cart and the CMU Rover", *Proceedings of the IEEE* **71**(7), 872–884. Also appeared in Cox & Wilfong (1990).

Moravec, H. P. (1984a), "Locomotion, Vision and Intelligence", in Brady & Paul, eds, *Proceedings of the First International Symposium on Robotics Research*, MIT Press, pp. 215–224.

Moravec, H. P. (1984b), Locomotion, Vision and Intelligence, in Brady & Paul, eds, *Robotics Research 1*, MIT Press, Cambridge, Massachusetts, pp. 215–224.

Moravec, H. P. (1987), "Sensor Fusion in Certainty Grids for Mobile Robots", in *IEEE Workshop on Mobile Robot Navigation Proceedings*.

Moravec, H. P. (1988), *Mind Children*, Harvard University Press, Cambridge, Massachusetts.

Nehmzow, U. & Smithers, T. (1991), "Mapbuilding using Self-Organising Networks in "Really Useful Robots"", in J.-A. Meyer & S. W. Wilson, eds, *Proceedings of the First International Conference on Simulation of Adaptive Behavior: From Animals to Animats*, MIT Press, Cambridge, Massachusetts, pp. 152–159.

Neumann, J. V. & Morgenstern, O. (1944), *Theory of Games and Economic Behavior*, John Wiley and Sons, New York, New York.

Newcombe, F. & Ratcliff, G. (1989), Disorders of Visupspatial Analysis, in *Handbook of Neuropsychology, Volume 2*, Elsevier, New York, New York.

Newell, A., Shaw, J. & Simon, H. (1957), "Empirical Explorations with the Logic Theory Machine", in *Proceedings of the Western Joint Computer Conference 15*, pp. 218–329. Also appeared in Feigenbaum & Feldman (1963) and Luger (1995).

Newell, A., Shaw, J. & Simon, H. (1958), "Chess Playing Programs and the Problem of Complexity", *Journal of Research and Development* **2**, 320–335. Also appeared in Feigenbaum & Feldman (1963).

Newell, A., Shaw, J. & Simon, H. (1959), "A General Problem-Solving Program for a Computer", *Computers and Automation* **8**(7), 10–16.

Newell, A., Shaw, J. & Simon, H. (1961), *Information Processing Language V Manual*, Prentice Hall, Edgewood Cliffs, New Jersey.

Nicolis, G. & Prigogine, I. (1977), *Self-Organization in Nonequilibrium Systems*, Wiley, New York, New York.

Nilsson, N. J. (1965), *Learning Machines*, McGraw-Hill, New York, New York.

Nilsson, N. J. (1971), *Problem-Solving Methods in Artificial Intelligence*, McGraw-Hill, New York, New York.

Nilsson, N. J., ed. (1984), *Shakey the Robot*, Stanford Research Institute AI Center, Technical Note 323.

Payton, D. W. (1986), "An architecture for reflexive autonomous vehicle control", in *IEEE Robotics and Automation Conference*, San Francisco, California.

Payton, D. W. (1990), "Internalized Plans: A Representation for Action Resources", *Robotics and Autonomous Systems* **6**(1,2), 89–103. Also appeared in Maes (1990*b*).

Pylyshyn, Z., ed. (1987), *The Robot's Dilema: The Frame Problem in Artificial Intelligence*, Ablex Publishing Corp., Norwood, New Jersey.

Raibert, M. H. (1986), *Legged Robots That Balance*, MIT Press, Cambridge, Massachusetts.

Raibert, M. H., Brown, H. B. & Murthy, S. S. (1984), 3-D Balance Using 2-D Algorithms, in Brady & Paul, eds, *Robotics Research 1*, MIT Press, Cambridge, Massachusetts, pp. 215–224.

Ramachandran, V. S. & Anstis, S. M. (1985), "Perceptual Organization in Multistable Apparent Motion", *Perception* **14**, 135–143.

Roberts, L. G. (1963), Machine Perception of Three Dimensional Solids, Technical Report 315, MIT Lincoln Laboratory.

Rosenblatt, F. (1962), *Principles of Neurodynamics*, Spartan, New York, New York.

Rosenschein, S. J. & Kaelbling, L. P. (1986a), "The synthesis of digital machines with provable epistemic properties", in J. Halpern, ed., *Proceedings of the Conference on Theoretical Aspects of Reasoning About Knowledge*, Morgan Kaufmann Publishers, Los Altos, California, pp. 83–98.

Rosenschein, S. J. & Kaelbling, L. P. (1986b), "The Synthesis of Machines with Provable Epistemic Properties", in J. Halpern, ed., *Proc. Conf. on Theoretical Aspects of Reasoning about Knowledge*, Morgan Kaufmann Publishers, Los Altos, California, pp. 83–98.

Rumelhart, D. E. & McClelland, J. L., eds (1986), *Parallel Distributed Processing*, MIT Press, Cambridge, Massachusetts.

Rumelhart, D., Hinton, G. & Williams, R. (1986), Learning Internal Representations by Error Propagation, in D. E. Rumelhart & J. L. McClelland, eds, *Parallel Distributed Processing*, MIT Press, Cambridge, Massachusetts, pp. 318–364.

Russell, S. J. (1989), "Execution Architectures and Compilation", in *Proceedings of the Eleventh International Joint Conference on Artificial Intelligence*, Morgan Kaufmann, Detroit, Michigan, pp. 15–20.

Sacks, O. W. (1974), *Awakenings*, Doubleday, New York, New York.

Samuel, A. L. (1959), "Some Studies in Machine Learning Using the Game of Checkers", *Journal of Research and Development* **3**, 211–229. Also appeared in Feigenbaum & Feldman (1963) and Luger (1995).

Sarachik, K. B. (1989), "Characterising an Indoor Environment with a Mobile Robot and Uncalibrated Stereo", in *Proceedings IEEE Robotics and Automation*, Scottsdale, Arizona, pp. 984–989.

Sejnowski, T. & Rosenberg, C. (1987), "Parallel Networks that Learn to Pronounce English Text", *Complex Systems* **1**, 145–168.

Selfridge, O. G. (1956), "Pattern Recognition and Learning", in C. Cherry, ed., *Proceedings of the Third London Symposium on Information Theory*, Academic Press, New York, New York.

Shannon, C. E. (1950), "A Chess-Playing Machine", *Scientific American*.

Shortliffe, E. H. (1976), *MYCIN: Computer-based Medical Consultations*, Elsevier, New York, New York.

Simmons, R. & Krotkov, E. (1991), "An Integrated Walking System for the Ambler Planetary Rover", in *IEEE Proceedings on Robotics and Automation*, Sacramento, California.

Simon, H. A. (1969), *The Sciences of the Artificial*, MIT Press, Cambridge, Massachusetts.

Slagle, J. R. (1963), A Heuristic Program that Solves Symbolic Integration Problems in Freshman Calculus, in E. A. Feigenbaum & J. Feldman, eds, *Computers and Thought*, McGraw-Hill, New York, New York, pp. 191–206. From a 1961 MIT mathematics Ph.D. thesis.

Slate, D. J. & Atkin, L. R. (1984), Chess 4.5–The Northwestern University Chess Program, in P. Frey, ed., *Chess Skill in Man and Machine*, Springer-Verlag.

Smith, B. C. (1991), "The Owl and the Electric Encyclopedia", *Artificial Intelligence Journal* **47**, 251–288.

Steels, L. (1990), "Towards a Theory of Emergent Functionality", in *Proceedings of the First International Conference on Simulation of Adaptive Behavior*, MIT Press, Cambridge, Massachusetts, pp. 451–461.

Steels, L. & Brooks, R., eds (1995), *The Artificial Life Route to Artificial Intelligence: Building Embodied, Situated Agents*, Lawrence Erlbaum Associates, Hillsdale, New Jersey.

Sussman, G. J. (1975), *A Computer Model of Skill Acquisition*, Elsevier, New York, New York.

Teitelbaum, P., Pellis, V. C. & Pellis, S. M. (1990), "Can Allied Reflexes Promote the Integration of a Robot's Behavior", in *Proceedings of the First International Conference on Simulation of Adaptive Behavior*, MIT Press, Cambridge, Massachusetts, pp. 97–104.

Thorpe, C., Herbert, M., Kanade, T. & Shafer, S. A. (1988), "Vision and Navigation for the Carnegie-Mellon Navlab", *IEEE Trans. PAMI* **10**(3), 362–373.

Tinbergen, N. (1951), *The Study of Instinct*, Oxford University Press, Oxford, United Kingdom.

Tsuji, S. (1985), Monitoring of a building environment by a mobile robot, in Hanafusa & Inoue, eds, *Robotics Research 2*, MIT, Cambridge, Massachusetts, pp. 349–356.

Turing, A. M. (1937), "On Computable Numbers with an Application to the Entscheidungsproblem", in *Proceedings of the London Math. Soc. 42*, pp. 230–265.

Turing, A. M. (1950), "Computing Machinery and Intelligence", *Mind* **59**, 433–460. Also appeared in Feigenbaum & Feldman (1963) and Luger (1995).

Turing, A. M. (1970), Intelligent Machinery, in B. Meltzer & D. Michie, eds, *Machine Intelligence 5*, American Elsevier Publishing, New York, New York, pp. 3–23.

Turk, M. A., Morgenthaler, D. G., Gremban, K. D. & Marra, M. (1988), "VITS–A Vision System for Autonomous Land Vehicle Navigation", *IEEE Trans. PAMI* **10**(3), 342–361.

Uexküll, J. V. (1921), "Ummwelt und Innenwelt der Tiere". Berlin, Germany.

Ullman, S. (1984), "Visual Routines", *Cognition* **18**, 97–159.

Viola, P. A. (1989), "Neurally Inspired Plasticity in Oculomotor Processes", in *1989 IEE Conference on Neural Information Processing Systems–Natural and Synthetic*, Denver, Colorado.

Viola, P. A. (1990), Adaptive Gaze Control, Master's thesis, Massachusetts Institute of Technology, Cambridge, Massachusetts.

Walter, W. G. (1950), "An Imitation of Life", *Scientific American* **182**(5), 42–45.

Walter, W. G. (1951), "A Machine That Learns", *Scientific American* **185**(5), 60–63.

Walter, W. G. (1953), *The Living Brain*, Duckworth, London, United Kingdom. Republished in 1961 by Penguin, Harmondsworth, United Kingdom.

Watkins, C. (1989), Learning from Delayed Rewards, PhD thesis, King's College, Cambridge, Cambridge, United Kingdom.

Waxman, A. M., Moigne, J. L. & Srinivasan, B. (1985), "Visual Navigation of Roadways", in *Proceedings of the IEEE Conference on Robotics and Automation*, St. Louis, Missouri, pp. 862–867.

Wehner, R. (1987), "'Matched Filters'–Neural Models of the External World", *Journal of Comparative Physiology* **A 161**, 511–531.

Wiener, N. (1948), "Cybernetics", *Scientific American* **179**(5), 14–19.

Wiener, N. (1961), *Cybernetics*, second edn, MIT Press, Cambridge, Massachusetts.

Wilkins, D. E. (1979), Using Patterns and Plans to Solve Problems and Control Search, Technical Report AI Memo 329, Stanford University.

Williams, M. R. (1983), "From Napier to Lucas", *Annals of the History of Computing* **5**(3), 279–296.

Wilson, D. (1966), "Insect Walking", Annual Review of Entomology, 11. 103–121.

Winograd, T. (1972), *Understanding Natural Language*, Academic Press, New York, New York.

Winograd, T. & Flores, F. (1986), *Understanding Computers and Cognition*, Addison-Wesley, Reading, Massachusetts.

Winston, P. H. (1972), The MIT Robot, in B. Meltzer & D. Michie, eds, *Machine Intelligence, 7*, John Wiley and Sons, New York, New York, pp. 431–463.

Winston, P. H. (1984), *Artificial Intelligence*, second edition edn, Addison-Wesley, Reading, Massachusetts.

Wood, W. B. (1988), "The Nematode *Caenorhabditis Elegans*", Cold Spring Harbor Laboratory. Cold Spring Harbor, New York.

Yap, C. (1985), Algorithmic Motion Planning, in J. Schwartz & C. Yap, eds, *Advances in Robotics, Vol. 1*, Lawrence Erlbaum Associates, Hillsdale, New Jersey.

Yarbus, A. (1967), *Eye Movements and Vision*, Plenum Press.